Walter B. Harris

Description of Satan's Court

treating the following subjects - a canvasser's dream - a grand council -

Satan makes a speech, giving the result of 6000 years' study of man -

exults at his success; the earth's crust is four miles thick

Walter B. Harris

Description of Satan's Court
treating the following subjects - a canvasser's dream - a grand council - Satan
makes a speech, giving the result of 6000 years' study of man - exults at his success;
the earth's crust is four miles thick

ISBN/EAN: 9783337301040

Printed in Europe, USA, Canada, Australia, Japan

Cover: Foto ©Lupo / pixelio.de

More available books at **www.hansebooks.com**

A DESCRIPTION

OF

Satan's Court

TREATING THE FOLLOWING SUBJECTS:

A Canvasser's Dream; A Grand Council; Satan Makes a Speech
Giving the Result of 6,000 Years' Study of Man; Exults
at His Success; The Earth's Crust is Four Miles Thick;
Inside it is Hollow; at the Poles are Large Open-
ings Through which Pass Vast Multitudes to
His Grand Auditorium; A Citizen of
Oakland Taken by a Friend to His
Majesty's Latest Grand Coun-
cil; A Grand Feast;
Toasts and Speeches.

ALSO

The Old Forty-Niner's Story.

By W. B. HARRIS.

INTRODUCTION.

DEAR READER:—Any port in a storm. I am old, penniless, and friendless. After an exceedingly active life, on the border, in the mountains, mining, or on plains, cattle and sheep-raising, I find myself at sixty years old in Oakland—broke. I have no means of a livelihood. In youth and early manhood I could devise a means of making money. Now, old and sick, I can do nothing but write a book. The storm of poverty and want is terrible. This is my only port, the writing of a book. A Christian gentleman, E. S. Fowler, goes my security to my publisher. He and others who heard my manuscript read, were good enough to call it very readable.

In the following pages the ground is taken that God and the devil have been in the world from Adam's creation, battling for character for their kingdoms. God with the Holy Spirit and the word of his truth endeavors to lead man up into a better and higher life. The position is taken that it is his privilege to go on learning of God in this world until he reaches a plane of happiness perfectly incomprehensible to the intellect of the unredeemed man. But man being totally depraved, and loving darkness rather than light, the devil, with his vast cunning and experience, has largely the advantage, and is peopling his kingdom more rapidly than God. He is in politics, shaping national measures to suit his purpose. He is in the courts, making judges follow old precedents to the enslavement of mankind. He is in all those Governments where the land is all in the hands of the few, and the common people are forced into the cities and towns, making the establishment and maintenance of standing armies necessary. He is an accomplished devil. He is better educated than any faculty of a college in the world; knows vastly more. He is perfectly accomplished in State craft. He has been able to cheat the United States for the last hundred years out of the realization of the most important facts which her history has developed, that is, that homes in the United States are the grand power upon which is based all modern civilization. The devil wants us to think that it is education, and he is constantly urging the country to educate the negroes and poor whites of the South, by some national provision looking to that end. Give the negroes homes, break up the system of land monopoly, all over the South, divide the land up among the inhabitants of the South, and education is sure to follow. I do not mean to rob the white people of their land, but tax land held in larger quantities than 160 or 300-acre tracts higher than any other property, and appropriate the money proposed for education to the buying of a home for a family, which money the family refund as fast as they become able. California is a splendid illustration of this matter; land monopoly covered every valley from San Diego to Shasta.

The State has had a splendid school fund from her earliest history, thanks to the United States Government. Its citizens have been forced into the different towns and cities, which have grown much faster than improvements in the country warranted. The schools have performed their duty, and now we already see the result in a generation of educated young men and women. In no State in this Union will you find so many young men in penitentiaries and jails. The places of honor and power are not in the hands of young men raised in the State. On the contrary, they are in the hands of young men raised in other States, or Ireland, or Germany.

Go to your churches on Sunday, and a large majority of the

men have gray beards, indicating an Eastern nativity. The young men raised and educated here are diminutive in mind and body.

The devil has cheated the State out of the million beautiful homes, which she ought to have had, and would have had, if the feudal land system, with the devil as chief council in the courts, had not won his cause against God and right and the best interest of the human race. It is a great deal easier for the devil to tear down a civilization that God and home and truth have been generations building up, than it is to build it. If we were to lose our homes in America, if land monopoly were established all over the United States as it is in California and Mexico, we would have a standing army to maintain law and order in less than ten years. The larger holdings are rapidly absorbing the smaller, and capitalists are having established a nucleus, around which will gather a standing army, and then our liberties are gone.

The devil is using another element to lower our civilization. A constant stream of low, cunning, unprincipled foreigners are flooding our land, filling our cities and towns. We must save our land for the Dutch and Irish and negroes that are here. We must legislate so as to make homes for our present homeless population. One man with a home, and under God educating his children, is a bulwark in favor of law and order and liberty. A hundred men loving lawlessness and disorder, who require ten or fifteen constables to look after them, will lower the civilization of a thousand. Our civilization is like a brook, flowing over a grassy plain, clear and beautiful. The emigration from foreign countries is a band of hogs wallowing in the brook, spoiling its waters.

SATAN'S COURT.

THURSDAY, JAN. 3, 1884.—Arose early with the view of canvassing Woodland for the *Prohibitionist;* when business opened, I commenced. I received the same or nearly the same answer from all: "No, I have all the papers I want." A great many said, "I favor the cause, but I think we will have a drought, and I must economize on every hand." No man put his hand in his pocket and said, "Yes, here is the money, you are engaged in a good fight and I will help you." At noon I was very tired and hungry. Ladies came to the door and said, "No, sir; we don't want it," and unceremoniously shut the door in my face in order to get back to their dinner. No one asked me to eat. I was genteelly dressed and looked more like a capitalist, than a poor old canvasser for a paper advocating an unpopular cause. At last hunger must be appeased; I had to walk a mile to a restaurant to get my dinner. So I watched closely, and finally I saw a Bible on a center table, and summoned courage to say, "Won't you let me have a little dinner? I am old and hate to walk a mile to a restaurant. She reluctantly fed me. After dinner I thought I would try farmers. So I started out. They looked upon me with evident scorn, and all declined to take my paper.

At night, footsore and tired, I approached the town of Cacheville. I called at the preacher's first. His wife met me at the door; I handed her a paper, at the same time taking a letter from Mr. Dunn, from a Bible and handing it to her, addressed "To all whom it may concern," stating my business, and recommending me to Christians; I was invited in, and rested my old, aching limbs a minute, when I was politely referred to Mr. Griffin, a leading member of the church. I observed it was sundown, and that I would go and see him. He received me at the door with courtesy, but did not invite me in. He was well dressed and had a fine house, evidently a man well-to-do. In answer to my usual inquiry, he said he was a prohibitionist, favored the cause, and did all he could for it and the church, but did not want my paper. I asked him to let me stay all night; he said, no, he was crowded and could not possibly accommodate me. I reasoned the case with him a little; he pulled out a half dollar and gave me; I put it down in my book as a subscription for three months to my paper; he did not want me to do so. I resolved not to take charity; he evidently wanted to make *me* the recipient of *his* alms. I was no beggar; I had ten dollars in my pocket. I did want to economize by paying a less price for food and lodging to a friend of the good cause than I would have to pay hotel-keepers. At the hotel I paid forty cents for a very poor supper, a poor man's day's wages. I got a bed at a private house and went to bed, completely worn out, at six o'clock, and terribly disgusted with California farmers. Not one cent had I taken in the whole day. I soon fell asleep and dreamed.

I had in my dreams, over and over again, the interviews of the day with the cold, hard-hearted, rich farmers. Their looks of superciliousness haunted me in my dream. I had interviewed a few suffering tramps during the day. Their worn, haggard, desponding looks also haunted my dreams. From out of this chaos my dreams took shape. I dreamed I was again a boy on the Chattahoochee River, Forsythe County, Georgia, with my old friend, Singleton Howell; he was, the last time I saw him, twenty-one years old, six feet high, and weighed 200 pounds. He had just fallen heir to a large farm, and over a hundred negroes. More than twenty families, poor white trash, were living off his bounty. He was as good as it was possible to be to his negroes. To be his property was the negro's paradise; but he was a terrible rake. Not less than forty children, black and white, pointed with lineaments unmistakable to him as their father. He was very popular with men and women. He drank just enough to be convivial. He was honored by a seat in the Legislature at twenty-two years of age, which place he exchanged only for a seat in Congress, in 1840.

Well, I dreamed that in front of the hotel in Cacheville I met a pale, haggard, shivering tramp, who surprised me by saying, " Billy [that is my name], give me a quarter to get a drink."

Looking up I beheld my old friend, Singleton Howell. "What," says I, extending my hand, but to my surprise there was no hand reached out to take mine. He did seem to glide off with my quarter, and I saw him take two glasses full of whisky and gulp it down. He again stood before me without walking in the street. Said I, "Are you a ghost?" he answered, "Yes." I said, "Tell me all about it." "Well," said he, "I was killed in the late war, and, of course, went straight to hell; but, Billy, I was a good man in this world, and I got a good place in hell. The devil gave me a place of high honor; but still it was hell. There was gnashing of teeth. There was wailing. There was the worm that dieth not. There was felt by all an eternal banishment from the presence of God, and all that was good. Strange to say, all my negroes that died went straight to Heaven. For a long time they shouted and sang, 'Glory to the Lamb,' but they seemed, after I was in hell about twenty years, to have a new arrival. I owned an old negro man who was incessantly boring me on religion. He would say, 'Massa, quit your sins, repent, and turn to Jesus; you are too good a man to go to hell; all are under condemnation without Jesus. But I laughed at him, and praised him, and gave him good clothes, and books, and his time. But he always worked. He did more work than two common men, and was the best singer I ever heard. Well, a thousand times I heard him praying for his poor massa. He had full charge of my place and property. One day he came to me and said: 'Massa, massa, Mr. Hammond whipped Jeff de odder day, and Jeff run away; he is a powerful good nigger, and is mighty anxious for you to buy him.' Said I, 'I have not got the money.' He answered, 'You borrow de money, and we will give in all hands and save enough on de crop extra to pay for him.' So I met Hammond in Warsaw that day and said, 'Has Jeff run away? he answered, 'Yes; and by God when I get him I'll whip him to death.' Said I, 'You are a d—d brute!' Well, you know we had had many a fight, Hammond and I. He knew I was the best man, and only said with set teeth, 'I'll shoot you, G— d— you, if you interfere between me and my niggers. You treat your niggers so well it spoils all the niggers in the neighborhood.' 'Well,' said I, 'come over to the hotel and take dinner with me;

I have wine, brandy, and everything.' I touched on his weak point; he came and drank heavily during the meal. I managed to steal his pistols, and hide them. He swore he would kill me. I humored his ferocious temper; we played cards, drank, caroused; got drunk ourselves, and made everything else drunk that we could. Hammond was terrible stingy, and when drunk wanted to gamble; but he had sworn never to gamble any more. Notwithstanding this I got him to gambling, and as he had no money I loaned him a hundred, which I soon won. Drink and avarice by this time had stimulated his appetite for gambling to the highest pitch. He asked for more money; I refused, unless he gave me security. I told him I would buy Jeff. He gnashed his teeth, and his ferocity was horrible; but passion and appetite favored me, and it all resulted in my holding a bill of sale of Jeff before morning.

"Well, I owned 300 negroes when the war broke out. Nearly 200 were procured pretty much in the foregoing manner through old Abe's influence. In the battle of Balls Bluff I was killed, and of course went to hell. I have been there twenty years. About a hundred of my negroes have died or been killed, and nearly all have gone straight to Heaven; their faith had saved them. As before remarked, there were many different places in hell. The devil honored me and gave me little devils for my servants. I had whisky and wine and gambling till I was tired to death of them. That kind of life had to last forever without change. Every man and woman continued the life they had led on earth. Whisky sellers seemed to have a worse life than any other class. Their bodies were swelled up to enormous proportions; they fed ravenously with an insatiable hunger, upon what they had robbed of helpless women and children. A great plant of a fiery color, smelling of brimstone, grew up from their feet, named WANT. They fed continuously, unceasingly, with awful unrest, terrible to look upon. Another class near them was the California farmer. A terrible lust for wheat and land and horses and carriages, and brag, consumed them. Also a fear, a horrible fear that a tramp would come along, made their eyes bulge out about an inch. They bragged from morning till night on their honesty and liberality. All this was never to end.

"Well, one day I was looking over to where a vast, countless multitude were singing and feasting, and shaking hands, and looking peaceful and happy. My eyes naturally wandered to my negroes, when I gazed in that direction. I was amazed to see them all going toward the banks of Jordan to meet some one; they looked very happy. What was my surprise to see old Abe, for it was him they were going to welcome. As was the general custom in paradise, all who had done good in the name of Jesus were welcomed ;by the recipients of their favors. I could not help but reflect how much better it was to be welcomed by a host on that side than have a fortune on the earth.

"Well, Abe was gladly greeted by that happy band; he was carried on angels' wings to the vast throng who surrounded the throne. Abe was very humble, and took a place where he thought he was very low. All at once a host of beautiful angels left the throne, and in a moment they surrounded old Abe, and placing their wings under him they gently lifted him and wafted him up, and bore him up to the feet of the Lamb. I then heard the words: 'He that abaseth himself shall be exalted. Enter thou into the joys of thy Lord.'

"Old Abe said, 'Lord, I prayed all my life for my young massa.' Just then his eyes fell upon me over in hell; without one word, he fell upon his knees. The command went forth that I was to have another chance on earth. So I started back on the road I went to hell, on through the grave. I had heard those cursed old Californians bragging so much, that, as I had my choice of places, I concluded to come here on the Sacramento River.

"Well, I landed here about two years ago, flat broke. What should I do? Hunger and thirst must be satisfied, and clothing must be had. I had never worked. I had no professional education. What should I do for a living? I wanted whisky, but had no money. I was back to reform, but somehow I could not believe on Jesus for me, even when I knew that he had saved millions of hosts. I thought I would lecture, but I could not get an audience. I thought I would keep men from selling whisky, as that was the worst hell, but they would not believe me. I worked for farmers, but I—Oh, it was terrific the life I have led,

and I am going back to hell; it is a much better place than it is
to be poor and friendless in California. Why, Billy, you keep
your trust. Obey the Scriptures, do good, make all happy whom
you meet, as you journey through life, and above all look every
moment to Jesus; and that which you enter upon by so doing is
better than gold, and lands, or houses, or merchandise. When
you die and go over yonder, hug and kiss old Abe for me; tell
him I thank him with all my heart; but there is no chance for a
poor old tramp in California to go to Jesus. The people here
have him all surrounded in fine churches, with fine clothing and
pomp and splendor. Tell Ábe I said it was better to be in hell
than to be here, and I am going back.

"What are you doing, Billy? Lend me another quarter? Billy,
what, are you canvassing for the *Prohibitionist* here among these
farmers? Well, I guess I won't take your quarter. Poor fellow,
I am awful sorry for you. A poor old quill-driving author, here
in California! To think that I, who am going back to hell,
should pity you! You will be happy forever, if you obey God;
but, my dear friend, the martyrs who were led to the stake with
great rusty chains eating into their flesh, had a better chance
than you. Good-bye, Billy—by the way I will take that quarter.
Nothing on earth is so exacting and imperious as whisky. When
our system gets well loaded, like a magnet the larger quantity
draws the smaller. The poor drunkard can feel the drink drawing him five miles. No wonder the saloon-keeper knows he has
a bill of sale of drunkards. Well, Billy, good-bye; I am going
to hell; I will see you across the gulf in Heaven if you are faithful." At this he glided into the hotel and took two more large
glasses of whisky.

He did this hurriedly. Setting down the glass the last time,
he took the bottle and turned it up to his mouth, and was rapidly
getting outside the contents, when I saw distinctly the bar-keeper
take a pistol from behind the counter, level it at my friend's heart,
and fire. The report of the pistol awoke me. The dream was
so vivid and impressive that I at once arose from my bed and
wrote it down. With the dream in my head, about 8 o'clock I
commenced canvassing the town. An interview with one man
will give the reader a correct idea of a day's work. The can-

vasser being told that Mr. K—— was a prohibitionist, and his house being pointed out, he repaired thither. He rang the bell.

The door was opened by Mrs. K——, a well-dressed, middle-aged lady.

Canvasser.—"I am working for the *Prohibitionist.* I want subscribers."

Lady.—"Yes, indeed; well, it is a cause that I think has God's sanction. I am a strong Prohibitionist."

Canvasser.—"Well, ma'am, won't you subscribe?"

Lady.—"Well, no; it's going to be a dry season, and we are carrying as many newspapers as we can."

Canvasser.—"Well, we are on the eve of a grand boom. Prohibition stock is going right up. The people all over the land are waking up. The enormous taxation arising from the trade in order to prosecute drunken criminals, and to feed them in jails, penitentiaries, and poor-houses, is the argument that reaches every tax-payer."

Lady.—"Yes; I am an old settler here, and know, of my own knowledge, of the loss of six splendid homes. You see that house, and that—" pointing to empty houses that stood in the distance. "I will tell you how that one was settled, and how the home was afterwards broken up; but come in."

The canvasser, being tired, thought he would rest and hear the story.

So the lady continued:—

"Mr. Turner, with four children, came across the plains in 1850, stopping first at what was then called Hangtown. He had six yoke of good oxen, and moved over here and took up that quarter-section of land. We took up this. He and his wife were from the border in Missouri. He was a good hunter and game abounded. Every pound that he killed was worth from two to four bits a pound. He bought a scythe and cut some hay, and hauled it over to Sacramento, getting as high as $100, and even $150 per load. Every time he went to town he got a little tipsy. In that condition he spent a fearful amount of money. He had no caution nor acquisitiveness, and very large friendship.

"The poor man loved his family, but the cruel bondage to whisky ruined him. In 1856 he sold his cattle and paid for his land. He had planted fruit trees and vines, and at that time was making wine. He went to the city with a load of hay. That saloon-keeper over in town met him in Sacramento, where they commenced drinking, and while drunk the saloon-keeper won his money, wagon, and team. When he sobered up the next morning, he felt so ashamed and miserable that he swore he, would drown himself. The saloon-keeper told him that if he would mortgage his farm for the money, he could take his team and go home with it. So it was agreed. They had a mortgage written by a lawyer and duly recorded in Washington, which was the county seat. After Turner's return home he was very miserable, keeping the above facts a secret from his wife, who was the hardest working woman I ever saw.

"I happened over there the day the saloon-keeper came for the money, and I shall never forget the deserted, ashy, forlorn look that spread over her face. She said: 'Whisky killed my poor mother and has made me and my children slaves. O God, if there is a God, this is three good homes I have helped that man to make, and I have worked, and saved, and patched, stayed at home and never went to church, and my children have never had anything to wear to school, and they are, just like I am, growing up in ignorance.' All these fine ranches," pointing toward other houses, "were first made by drinking men, who got in debt and had to sell. Whisky is the mortal enemy of homes."

That evening I returned to Sacramento and was ordered to Oakland.

I came to Oakland Monday, January 7, 1884, to canvass for the *State Prohibitionist.* I was to get for my work $1.00 per day and board, and an interest in the paper in case we built it up and made it a valuable property.

Oakland was known as the "City of Churches." It was the seat of the State University. The wealth and taste of the whole Pacific Coast had been lavished upon its improvements. There were more beautiful residences and well improved grounds than in any place I had ever seen. San Francisco, with all her millionaire merchants, had come over here to build among the old oaks residences in which to spend, with wife and children, their last years on earth. Any one would say that it was a good field to work for such a cause. I began about 9 o'clock on Eighth Street, intending to go over the whole city street by street. At every house it was about the same, " No," or " No, sir." I was a pretty decent-looking old gentleman, working for my own paper— an honorable calling. What was the matter? Monday, Tuesday, Wednesday all passed with the same result.

I had always had terrible pluck and energy, and unbounded faith in any of my well matured plans. I began to get scared. Is my brain softening? Have I got to work in the wrong cause? A hundred persons wished me success every day in my labors. Should I give up the battle and beat a hasty retreat and go back to Sacramento? About an average of one a day, after hard trying, for three weeks. What was I to do? Work till I was very tired, sit up till midnight writing a pamphlet to publish, which I wanted to sell that I might get bread and butter. On the eighteenth day of January I worked hard with poor luck; attended meeting at the headquarters of the Salvation Army, went with feeble steps to my lonely room, and wrote with throbbing brow, till midnight.

When I sadly retired to my virtuous couch I could not sleep. I again interviewed beautiful, richly dressed women, rang door bells, and was terribly nauseated with politeness.

Suddenly my dream took shape. My old friend Singleton Howell was again troubling my dreams, but very different this time from his appearance before.

I dreamed that I went to a large and costly church in Oakland. I was shown to a seat in the back part of the church by the usher. Although well dressed, I imagined all eyes were turned upon me on account of my failure to come up to the fashionable standard. I dreamed that I was trying to get into a devout frame of mind. When the preacher arose, what was my surprise to see in the tall, well dressed, sanctimonious divine, my old friend Singleton Howell. I dreamed that he read, in a most resonant voice, a beautiful hymn, which was sung by the richest-looking choir I had ever seen.

The preacher, standing, prayed most thrillingly. Says I, " What is it? I am dreaming," but I could not awake. When he arose he took for his text:—

" Get thee behind me, Satan, for it is written thou shalt not live by bread alone, but by every word that proceedeth out of the mouth of God."

I knew that preacher was my old friend, Singleton Howell, that he was a ghost, and that he had been dead and in hell twenty-two years; that as a particular providence he was allowed once more to return to earth that he might embrace Christ; that after trying about two years in California, he had concluded the task an impossible one for a tramp, and had concluded to return to the place from whence he came as being preferable for a penniless tramp to this. The church, I dreamed, was the most costly structure I had ever seen of its kind. The audience was the finest dressed and most cultured in appearance I had ever seen in my life. I imagined that there were the marks of fast living upon the countenances of all, both old and young. An indulgence in fine wines had forced to the surface of many fair cheeks and brows, blue veins that would otherwise have sought to flow in a more hidden channel.

The preacher, six feet high, a perfect specimen of manhood, with a very large head and symmetrical features, except the mouth, which was very large; his voice, peculiar and resonant, so perfectly trained that every person in that vast audience caught every intonation.

There was perfect self-abandon. He stood towering, motion-less, at first pale, but as he proceeded the color deepened. Such a flow of electric oratory I had never heard, as he pictured fallen man at the mercy of a foe who possessed perfect knowledge of man's weaknesses, and had been practicing his arts on man from the day of Adam's fall. By nature an alien from God, and with this powerful foe to mislead and tempt with such power. He then, after a long pause, turned to the great deliverer, Christ, and, with manner and eloquence, electrified the whole audience. He begat an emotional tension almost painful to bear.

His sermon lasted one hour. At its close he said, "Let us pray." He leaned forward, and with a perfect pathos appealed to Heaven for help against so powerful an enemy. At its close he said, "Sing the doxology." The congregation arose, and, being dismissed, they seemed spell-bound. The preacher walked through the aisles shaking hands. I remained standing also. He made his way to where I stood, and with both his he caught my hand and said, "Come to my room to-night," leaving a twenty-dollar gold piece and his card in my hand.

On leaving the church I immediately sought a restaurant and satisfied my hunger.

I was very impatient for the hour to arrive, as the reader may imagine.

At nine o clock I knocked. The door was opened by Singleton himself. He embraced me very affectionately and led me into a splendidly furnished apartment, in the center of which was a table covered with all the delicacies of the season, brandy, whisky, wine and everything that could tempt the appetite. Two ladies lounged voluptuously upon a sofa, to whom he introduced me, as his oldest and best friend. I saw plainly that they had been waiting for me, for they pulled a chair out from the table, bidding me be seated. When we were all seated, Singleton poured from a bottle a glass of wine for each, and said, "Billy, drink to the health of my king." I bowed, and blushed, and stammered, and drank. They all did the same. "Now," said he, "I am burning to gratify your curiosity." I now saw they were all full of wine, and he wanted to talk, so he commenced. "You know that saloon-keeper shot me, and you awoke, well that was all true. I vanished when he pulled the trigger. It scared the saloon-keeper to death. He immediately embraced religion, and I suppose he will go to Heaven. I dropped my humanity and went back to hell, I confess a little ashamed of myself. Spirits have only to will it, and in a second they travel millions of miles. I saw a vast multitude gathered together as I approached my old quarters. I will say to you, for your better understanding, that there is no law of gravitation in that place. A spirit flying through ether with the rapidity of thought can instantly stop, fold his wings, and rest on ether. There is no atmosphere. When you speak, your voice travels millions of miles in a moment. Well, I was met on my approach by a vast multitude of the inhabitants. A leader stepping to the front took off his hat, and, bowing low, said that he was profoundly honored by being the bearer from his majesty of welcome news to you, sir. We have gotten up in honor of your return, the grandest reception ever known in Hades.

2

You were the first man ever released from this place and allowed to return to earth, and have one more chance of getting to Heaven. And furthermore, sir, you are the first man that ever voluntarily took up his line of march for this country. When you were talking to that old canvasser in Cacheville, imps of his majesty heard you and instantly reported your conversation. He ordered an ovation. Not a soul in all his majesty's vast domain but will be here to witness your triumphant return. I am Cain who killed my brother, and of course I am the oldest settler from earth, in this country, and I never saw a man who did not have to be brought here in chains. Just listen to the clanking chains. They wear them forever.

"Just then there was an immense scattering or parting in the vast multitude, and his majesty himself appeared. He called me to him. I approached him. He caught me to his breast and shed great tears over me. Said he, 'There is all the vast throng that Noah preached to, and who would not repent there in Nineveh. There is Sodom and Gomorrah. There are the wicked children of Israel who fell in the desert. In a word,' said he, 'all the nations that forget God are here.' [I had drank, in my dream, a whole bottle of wine, and he pointed to the brandy and we begun on that.]

"We could see over into Heaven, where there were vast multitudes, but incomparably smaller than the multitudes surrounding his majesty. A great feast was prepared in my honor. Speeches were made by men who lived before the flood, enumerating the very few means then employed to deceive men and make them worship idols. God was jealous, and that nation which engaged in idolatrous worship was allowed to follow it up in hell to all eternity. There were speeches made by a large number of old Jews, describing the manner used by his majesty's servants to lead them from the true worship. His majesty himself made a speech, heard plainly by every inhabitant of his dominion. I will give you a brief synopsis of his speech.

SATAN MAKES A SPEECH.

" 'I have earnestly studied man's weak points from his creation. God has often given me great trouble. He at first put into man a disposition to worship. I soon learned to take every advantage of that by flattering their vanity. I could always delude them into erecting an altar to some other God. Before the taking possession of Canaan by the Israelites, I had it pretty much my own way. He then made a law that beat me.

" 'That was this. He divided the land up into inheritances, or homes, that had an effect on the human head and heart that was always too much for me. You see they were placed in a condition, the home condition, that naturally improved them. It made them loyal to God, and country, and virtue, and I always draw off all my forces when I find the land in any country divided up into homes. It was that condition that made the civilization of Egypt. She arose to be the granary of the world. Well, I filled Jerusalem and the cities of ancient Egypt with wine and beautiful women and idols, so that when the young men of the homes full of love to God and virtue, went on business to the cities, they went back intoxicated with the idea of leading a city life. They would sell out and move to the city, and soon get to loving wine and women, and finally worshiping the gods that I had ingeniously contrived to have introduced along with foreigners. You see the heathen were there on account of the increased prosperity occasioned by these homes.

" 'You see as soon as homes were established, that is, every head of a family owned what land he could make productive, they would build school houses and churches, and work, and study the resources of their land, and fight for their homes. But just let me get them away to the city, and they would lose the improvement in a week or two that it took a generation to build up. The great power of the Romans was built up on the home condition. The learning and wisdom of the Greeks had the home condition as a foundation. God made that a law of nature, just as he made gravitation a material law.

" 'On the decline of the Roman Empire, I induced the Gauls to make war on the tribes and nations in the south of Europe. When they conquered a province, they took possession of it in favor of the prince, and he divided the land up into large tracts, among his most renowned followers. The common people had no homes; they belonged to the soil, and when the land passed from one owner to another, they, the common people, went with

it. That was called the Feudal Land System. That system completely destroyed the plans of God; not but what a few poor
people always looked to Jesus.   I never could get entire control;
but I brought about the Dark Ages, which lasted nearly sixteen
centuries; and if it had not been for my neglect, I could have
kept mankind in just that condition.'   Here the devil tore his
hair and grew wrathful at the thought of his want of vigilance.

" ' I was busily engaged in other parts when Sir Walter Raleigh
gave to six hundred immigrants a home each, in case they would
remain and cultivate the soil.   There is where I made the greatest mistake of my life.   This was at Jamestown, State of Virginia.
They concluded to accept the offer, and when they did, they
called into being a power which had been dead twenty centuries,
and in spite of all my determined cunning, has been the cause of
all modern civilization in the world.

" ' I cannot touch one of God's laws.   It is a law that when a
man looks to Jesus, he is saved.   If he looks to him all the time,
he is perfectly saved.

" ' So you see these people built school houses and churches,
and met together and worshiped God.   He was well pleased and
had all power, and blessed them and prospered them as no people
ever did prosper.   Under the home power I could do nothing.
They rapidly raised up a superior people, purified by the Lord,
and zealous of good works.   It took only a hundred and fifty
years to raise up Washington and his armies.

" ' Then followed the establishment of the great American
Republic.   I was terrified.   What could I do ?   Here was progress, and I could do nothing to prevent it.

" ' Then followed that generation which made so many new
inventions.   When the cotton gin was discovered, I thought I
could take a grand advantage of it by fastening, like a festering
sore, slavery upon that people forever; but the Southern planters
were good men and Christians, actually bettering the condition of
their negroes.   Of course I got a few Yankees, Englishmen, and
Irishmen who went down South and brutally treated their negroes,
like Dick Hammond.

" After an area of great prosperity the Mexican War came on,
and the United States acquired Texas, New Mexico, Arizona,

and California, all covered with large land grants. That was just into my hand, and I have been reaping a good harvest ever since.

"'Then when the War of the Rebellion came on, I managed so that nearly all the land in the United States worth having should fall into the hands of land monopolists, and now, if the devil has not lost his cunning, the United States will go back into barbarism yet.' Cheers rang out, the chains rattled, thunders rolled, lightning flashed, and all hell seemed writhing in flames.

"Order was soon restored, when he continued:—

"'Now God released you [addressing me] from hell in answer to the prayer of that accursed old nigger, Abe, and gave you another chance to embrace Jesus. You failed to do so, for reasons of your own. I honor you for your good sense, and now it is my time to send you back to earth. [Loud applause.] I shall send you back as a preacher. I want you to preach in all the cities of the earth, beginning at Oakland.' So preparations were made for my immediate return to earth, in the service of his Satanic majesty. Prior to my arrival a report was circulated that a very talented young divine from London would preach in such a church on a certain Sunday.

"Well," I asked, "how did you promote the interest of the devil by such a sermon?"

"Mankind are responsible for every word of truth they hear. If they allow truth to take root in their hearts, then they are blessed and made happy by it. If not raised up by the reception of truth and brought into a better life, it stands against them all along the journey of life. He hardens his heart against this truth, and against that, day after day, through his whole life. At the last day they all rise up and he sees them standing there, and he says, 'Oh, miserable man, how did I make such mistakes? Now I see I have chosen to fix my own destiny. I did not choose Christ as my portion, and will now have to spend an eternity in making mistakes. I rejected the truth, and now I shall always be rejecting it.'"

Where do you preach next?"

"In —— Church to-morrow, in San Francisco. Here, Billy, is a check for $1,000. Honor me by your presence every time I preach. I am anxious to have the press in attendance when I preach. My sermon has been telegraphed all over the land. I know you are poor, but I have orders from the devil to put just as many such men as you are to work as soon as possible."

"Well," said I, "my dear friend, I don't understand you. You put me in surroundings where the senses are all captivated; you make me drunk; you give me $1,000 and then boldly announce that you have orders to put me to work for the devil, your master."

I smelled brimstone burning, and heard the clanking of chains. A great ugly worm dropped from the ceiling upon the table. It was the worm that dieth not. Singleton and the women laughed loud and long. Their laughter was echoed from interminable dungeons. I said to Singleton, "Is this hell?" He answered, "Yes." I said, "God have mercy in the name of Jesus." In a moment all was quiet and my fears were dispelled. I moved to throw the worm off the table and kill it, but he restrained me. "You kill that worm and countless thousands will spring from its remains. They live on the heart-strings of the people; they get fastened on around the heart in this life; they gnaw and eat and fatten, and never, *never*, NEVER let go in time nor eternity. All the world over they abound, and he who fails to get rid of them in life carries a multitude of them throughout the vast cycles of eternity."

"Why, how do they get rid of them?"

"By calling on the name of Jesus. He said he would be found of all those who called upon him, even though he be afar off."

I dropped on my knees, and, with throbbing heart, said, "I thank God for Jesus Christ, thy son, whose blood cleanseth me, even me."

In a moment the room was cleared of the women and the feast.

I said, "Here, Singleton, take back this check; it has worms on it and I won't have it."

"Why, said he, "I do not want you to change your business. You are doing God's work, but my master is reaping the benefit of it."

"Why," said I, "how is that?"

"Well, you are old, and poor, and decrepit, perhaps hungry and in need of medicine. You approach a very fine residence and ring the bell. A lady in rich attire opens the door. You say at once, 'I am working for the *Prohibitionist.*' She says, 'We don't read it,' and shuts the door. There is a worm in that woman's heart. Already is ringing in her ears, ' For I was hungered, and ye gave me no meat; I was thirsty, and ye gave me no drink; was in prison, and ye visited me not.' You go to a Christian with rich surroundings and present your cause. He says, 'I have all the papers that I can carry or read. I am doing all I can for prohibition and the church.' He does not say, 'Here, lose no time with me; take a dollar or two and send me the paper. I can give it to somebody, if I don't read it.' You slowly take your departure. That man has a worm. He hears deep down in his heart the voice of the meek and lowly one, 'Inasmuch as ye did it not to one of the least of these ye did it not to me. Go away into everlasting punishment.' On the other hand, he who with open arms receives and invites you in to rest, hospitality beaming on his features, and who says, 'Yes, your work is God's work; how much is your paper? $2.00; that is high.' 'Well,' you say, 'We issue 5,000 copies a week. Our subscription is 400. The 4,600 we give away whenever we can find a man to read it.' 'All right; here is your $2.00. God bless you. Amen.' You wring his hand, take your departure, and leave that man with a voice singing in his heart these words, ' I was a stranger, and ye took me in; I was naked, and ye clothed me; sick and in prison, and ye visited me.' Now, Billy, how many have you visited since your arrival?"

"About a thousand."

"Well, I suppose you have left a worm in the hearts of 990. If you won't take the check I will manage to see you and keep your wants supplied. But it is to the devil's interest that you should be in want, that you should let your wants be known, that they should positively refuse to relieve you. If they do not go out and hunt up the want and relieve it, they will get the worm that never dieth in their hearts. I preach to-morrow in —— Church. Hark! Do you hear that? His majesty summons me to his presence. Come and go with me; I will bring you back safe."

He caught me in his arms and before I could remonstrate we were in an intolerable cold region.

"We are passing the North Pole now, Billy."

It all of a sudden got hot.

"We have now entered hell. You see the crust of the earth is only about four miles thick, and all inside is hollow. In this place the devil holds his court. We will go slow now, so that I can explain what we see. The lesson learned will be invaluable to you in the world in which you live. There are the people whom Noah preached to. They are as happy as barbarians are in your world. An opportunity lost follows a man through vast eternity. They were not bad people and are not much punished. They lead, you see, the same kind of lives they led on earth. There are all the vast heathen nations of ancient and modern times, in fair hunting-grounds. Here are all the tribes of Israel after Moses' time and up to the coming of Christ. Opportunity improved made for those people the character that qualified them for Heaven. The same opportunity slighted put them into a hell a degree hotter than barbarism. Jesus provided a great salvation, the bare neglect of which was sufficient to consign men to torment. I was full of the salvation of Jesus. I was good to everybody. The condition of 300 negroes was greatly elevated and blessed by me. A large number of white men, women, and children knew where to get corn at my crib. They cultivated my land without paying rent. My forefathers had been followers of the meek and lowly, and I inherited very large veneration and benevolence. I committed only one sin, and that was the neglect of so great a salvation. If I had got out of that battle alive, I would have embraced Jesus and preached to the soldiers, but procrastination made me put it off just a little too long, and I got shot. You see that vast army of well-dressed men, cultured and well educated? What would you suppose was their calling? They are preachers and priests. They were pretty good men, representing all generations from Christ to the present. God says, 'Son, give me thine heart.' These preachers did not do it, and here they are, preaching forever, just as they did on earth. Their incessant preaching gets to be an intolerable punishment and they realize the terrible mockery in their hearts. But now we come to a vast multitude engaged in accumulating vast quantities of a filthy stuff they imagined was money. They gathered on and on, looking enviously on each other's piles, trading, trading. Their punishment was terrible. The drunkard was classed with a vast multitude of lunatics. The manufacturers and venders of alcohol came last. They were in a vast field where a plant grew about as high as their heads. It was the color of a flame of fire. A smoke that smelled of brimstone went up from it. Its name was WANT. They ate it ravenously, their cheeks bulged out and hung down. Their paunches almost dragged the ground. There they fed on this plant, gathering it in from both sides and cramming it into their insatiable maw. A burning thirst consumed them, while a beautiful clear stream seemed to flow at their feet. Its rippling music made them go wild with want.

Said I, "Singleton, take me back to earth."

"Oh, we have come to attend a grand council, and here we are."

We were in the presence of his majesty, the devil. He called all the vast multitude to order. He thundered reports from the world. Everything from Europe, Asia, and Africa was all that could be desired. In South America and Mexico the feudal land system had fixed everything permanently as well as could be desired. But the great contest was in the United States. In that country was the commencement of the grandest struggle the world had ever witnessed. One billion dollars in whisky—the industry of a million men. Land and railroad monopoly was now king.

His majesty arose and said, "My allies and friends," bowing low (he was as polite as the ladies and gentlemen of Oakland), "the whisky business is doing splendid work for me. Land monopoly is on our side. We are flooding the country with a pauper immigration from Europe, which has already greatly lowered the general level of civilization. In several States we have repealed the Sunday law, but the best stroke ever made is to come. We have succeeded in banishing the Bible from the public schools all over the land. I never could do anything with a man who read the Bible in his school-boy days. Another very prominent feature is this: The preachers are very learned and eloquent, and describe, in most eloquent terms, the goodness and love of God, but never say a word about me or hell. They do not honor me with a thought; but don't I wake them up when God, in his wrath for their failure to declare the truth, says, ' Depart ye cursed.' They do not want such men in Heaven, and I don't want them here, and I would be very glad to give them a supply of fire and brimstone with which to start a little hell of their own. They would try to burn each other up. See them, how they are preaching now. All denominations are there firing away at each other. Singleton Howell, I make you chief of the American delegation. Homes in that country are my greatest enemies and Heaven's strongest ally. Now whisky, alcohol, is our best friend, for we cannot attack these homes with any other weapon. Get a man to dram drinking, and then, when under the influence of drink, start a horse race or a game of cards. Loan him money and make him think that he is the smartest man in the world. By and by, as a matter of business, take a mortgage on his farm, and then the home is broken up, and he and his wife and children belong to me. The man who buys a farm becomes a land monopolist, and wants more and more, and through greed I shall get him. You must preach in all the cities and towns of California. Dwell particularly in praise of the rich State and liberal people. They would swallow a lie in that line backward, if they had to do it against scales as big as those on my back. Look at them. I can make them happy by calling them rich and liberal even here in hell. They all come here on account of their greed. In your sermons elevate the wine interest. That is our best friend. I will ruin all California's fairest homes yet. Oratory is better than gold. Let it be known that you are from London; that you had been traveling on the continent for the last four years, carefully arranging statistics in reference to temperance, and that, according to the best accounts, there was almost no drunkenness in those countries where wine was cheap and abundant, and that no crime in such countries was traceable to drunkenness; that Jesus of Nazareth had made wine, and that it was just as much a blessing as flour made from wheat, or clothing made from cotton. I will send out 1,000 servants, who are to report to you, and you will give them such orders as you think best. Remember that habit makes character, and that character fixes destiny. Get every man to join the church. But here I give you a lotion called 'Secure, now, safe. No use to do any more; I belong to the church.' Above all, waste no time. I have studied man for six thousand years. There are large numbers of men and women in the world who, when converted, turned right away from their sins and have since honestly taken all pains possible to know their duty to God, to country, to family, and to society. God leads such people. Just let them alone; it is time thrown away to fool with them. Their hearts are full of love to God and man. They are modest, unassuming, tender-hearted, always abounding in works of charity and love. They are perfectly saved and perfectly kept by the power of God's love shed abroad in their hearts. Lose no time with such people. Old Abe was just such a man. He did all the good possible in the world. When he was called over to the other side, not less than a thousand people met him on Jordan's banks. They had been recipients of his favors in the world. When he arrived in sight of the Lamb he fell down and worshiped away off, but angels surrounded him, lifted him up, and bore him to the side of the risen Saviour. Don't bother such men. You will have plenty to do. In all the churches you will find preachers who are long-winded, and who talk and preach a great deal. Encourage them. Flatter them. Make them think that every time they open their mouth fountains of wisdom uninterruptedly flow. They will soon kill any church, and then a dose or two of the lotion, which you must never be without, will put a whole church to sleep. Then there is a class of long-faced, speech-making old men and women in every church. Take a great deal of pains with them. Stimulate their avarice. Put good sound arguments into their minds against ever doing an act of charity; and in case they should give of their abundance a little to some poor woman, make them boast of it till they tire their neighbors to death. In every meeting make them take all the time. Always be stimulating the self-esteem of such. Make them think their presence is absolutely necessary at every testimony meeting. Then induce two or three to get up and take all the time, and keep such always in the way of young convert's testimony. If they testify, by all means make them testify of crooked paths and shortcomings. That is testifying for us. Don't ever let any man or woman get up and say, ' I am trusting in Jesus and am glad to know when I am in the line of intelligent duty, for God puts in my heart the sweetest happiness when I, in his name, discharge my duty.' Crowd such out with the long-winded talking old men and women. Then there is the Salvation Army and holiness bands, who throw precious pearls before swine. Just let them alone; they are doing us no harm. They may get to Heaven themselves, and I think they will. At least I don't want them here. They have money, and say it is the Lord's, but they seem to think it is a great deal better for them to keep it for the Lord than to invest it in his name. Then there is in all the towns and cities a vast army of poor. Make them dissatisfied. Keep them away from churches on account of their clothes. They are generally better educated and more refined than their rich neighbors and would enjoy the sermon and the worship, but they can barely keep soul and body together, much less decently go to chnrch. Put cankering envy in their hearts. Fill their mouths with useless complaints. Keep in mind character is what we want. Every man, woman and child is engaged in making the character which must live forever."

God is in the world at every single point, and has always been just the same as he was when he made it, and is always ready to lead man into a new life. God put into man a little of himself, when he made him, and it was that which became alienated by disobedience. That part of man will never die. If it commences an obedient trusting life in this world, it will be led out in a beautiful life, fit to live with God and the angels forever. If it does not yield obedience, then it is ours; make it useful. Then there is another class, the rich and well-to-do, of whom there are vast numbers in San Francisco and Oakland. Fifty or one hundred of that class arrive every day. There is one now, a finely dressed lady, in a splendid buggy drawn by a noble looking horse. A scroll is in front of the buggy on which is written in large letters, " Judgment is sure. My judgment will overtake thee." A fortune of $50,000, well invested, yielding an income of $6,000 per annum. A church letter from the M. E. Church of Oakland certifying that she was an acceptable member of the church. She had a fine house and grounds. In youth she gave her heart to God and was very happy; but she gradually allowed selfishness and pride and vanity to absorb her every thought. There they stood condemning her; all the truth scorned that she had ever heard stood in mourning by her side. She had her money all along with her, crushing her soul. Here were a hundred women pleading for washing, the very hardest drudgery, to keep starvation from their children, surrounding her buggy. No; John Chinaman does my washing, and does it well and cheaply; I cannot change. In the twenty years of her womanhood a hundred tramps had begged a scrap at her door. There was nothing cooked, not a scrap.

An asthmatic old man had asked a subscription for the *Prohibitionist*. No; I cannot afford it. There his ghost was appearing, saying, Opportunity lost. The worms in her heart made her utter the most heart-rending moans. Want stalking abroad in Oakland. Poor, destitute women walk the streets all night without shelter, cold and hungry. Many had looked to God through Jesus, and their sins, which were many, were all blotted out. The ghost of every one of these stood by her buggy, and on their bodies was written, "Ye did it not unto one of the least of these."

"Oh," said she, "too late, too late!" in reply to a voice she had heard ten thousand times in life, which said, "Son, give me thine heart." The cry would go up forever, "Too late, too late." She looked over and saw me and knew me, and said, "I saw you in Oakland. You are not as I am, dead, and your judgment along with you; you yet live. Tell every one in Oakland that 'Habit makes character and character fixes destiny,' as Mr. Dunn often said. Tell them that the first step is to get rooted in the vine, the true vine, and then, oh, such beautiful clusters of fruit gather around the vine, as they travel through life, which live forever. Tell them not to lose an opportunity of doing good; if they do, it makes a worm, that grows up before their eyes, and is named after the opportunity lost, and which never dies. And they bring all their money with them, and that which was called for by some suffering one on earth is put in a sack and hung around their neck, marked with the lost opportunity, in letters of fire. Now, suppose one has a $50,000 fortune and $5,000 income saved for twenty years as I had, and an opportunity of doing good that

would have used it all. True I did no harm; I was a lady of
fashion; but alas, alas! here I am, here I am, unutterably miserable forever, forever, on account of opportunity lost!"

While this panorama was going on before my eyes, the devil
had ordered a grand feast. The tables extended from pole to pole
right through the earth; everything that the mind was capable of
thinking about was there; but the worm that never dieth was in
everything. All were seated, I with the others, but I did not eat.
I was pressed to drink of the wine or brandy, but I declined.
They strained all the worms out and offered me a glass of nectar
a thousand years old, but I would not. They feasted and drank
till they were all drunk; large numbers were under the table. The
table was cleaned off in an instant. "Toasts and speeches are
now in order, said his majesty."

Singleton Howell arose with his glass filled to the brim.
Said the devil, " Fill your glasses to drink to Mr. Howell's toast.
He is my most honored subject on account of being the first man
who ever came here voluntarily. Here's to the health of the
reverend Mr. Thomas." Mr. Thomas arose and said: " Your
majesty and fellow subjects, I was born in the good old State of
Missouri. My father and mother were old hardshell Baptists. I
was raised up in that faith (I don't believe I ought to be here).
I joined the Baptist Church (the old side) by experience. My
experience was this, and it was sufficient. I told them that I had
given myself to God; to his service as long as I lived; and by the
authority of God's word I was his child as soon as I went down
into the water and was immersed, or baptized, in the name of the
Father, Son, and Holy Ghost. Well, I was soon after licensed
to preach. I baptized a great number into the church. I did all
I could for God and the church. I worked hard all the week,
made money, preached on Sunday, and was very happy in the
service of God. I gave cheerfully and largely of my money, and
oh, I do wish I had died before I was forty years old, in Missouri!
At twenty-two I married a well made, beautiful woman. We
had, in Missouri, twelve children, in twenty years. In 1849 we
immigrated to California. Oh, what a mistake ! We arrived in
Hangtown with five wagons and teams and one hundred head of
loose cattle and twenty-five good horses and mules, in September,

1849. I had about a thousand dollars. I built a log house in Hangtown, put my family into it, and with my team made a trip to Sacramento. There I bought supplies of provisions and a barrel of whisky. My father always kept it and I had. When I drove up to my door in Hangtown, my oldest son met me at the door and said, ' Dad, did you bring any whisky?' 'Yes,' said I. 'Well,' said he, 'there ain't none in this town. It is worth fifty cents a drink. There are a hundred men here waiting for you. 'Old Thomas has whisky,' yelled half a dozen voices. 'I bought it for my own use, boys.' 'Here is fifty cents; give me a drink. I drew it for him; he said, 'take a pinch of that gold-dust. I kept on drawing that whisky, till it was all gone. I weighed my gold-dust, and the barrel brought me $2,000. The boys had sold my provisions and tools for $2,000 more. You see I made $3,000 clear on the trip. I immediately made another trip, returning in four days. Other teams had arrived with provisions, tools, and whisky; and so I started a hotel and bar. Well, I rented ten tables at $10.00 a day each to gamblers, to play on. I built a large cloth house for a hotel. No man ever came along in those days asking for a miner's outfit but what he got it, money or no money. There was three or four hundred of my old neighbors and neighbor's sons in my neighborhood. They came in and weighed their dust on my scales every night. The diggings were rich and they took out vast quantities of gold. My receipts were $1,000 per day. My old neighbors drank and gambled. I wondered at it, for I did not. A great many of my old friends had left their families in great distress, in order that they might get an outfit, promising to send back money as fast as they earned it. But they drank their money up at my bar, or gambled it off in my house. I was thoroughly disgusted with them, and when they would come in Saturday night and drink all night and spend their money, and carouse all day Sunday, I soon got to throwing them out and driving them off. I was big and strong, and the more I threw out the more I wanted to. Well, I made money very fast. I put up a very large gambling hall. It was filled night and day. I owned an interest in several tables, having furnished the house, tables, and banking capital.

" My old Brother Smith, a good Baptist preacher, struck a

rich pocket and took out $10,000. His family was exceedingly destitute. He came into the store, his countenance all lit up, thanking God for his good luck. He treated and I treated. He commenced bragging on his skill as a miner, and I praised him. He treated, and, finally losing all caution, commenced gambling. He drank and gambled until he lost all, at one of my banks. I was mad at him and abused him. He took it all for a day or two, begging whisky and his meals, till I finally threw him out of the door. I did that to a great many, fifty or seventy-five, in the next two years. Well, one day in a great row, I got shot dead. At that time I had $200,000 or more. Well, I started to Judgment. I thought I was sure of Heaven. I had preached and baptized. My doctrine, once a child of God, always, came into my mind. True, I had not prayed for two years. I was too busy; I had given good advice every day to my old neighbors: it was none of my business if they did not take it. Well, when I started, it looked to me as if an army of men, women, and children clustered around me and went with me.

" Here was Brother Smith and an aged father and mother, and a large family. Brother Smith had never saved a dollar since I had robbed him at my bar and bank. The starving family with all their suffering, had written in letters of fire, ' Woe unto him who putteth the cup to his neighbor's lip.' A thousand men who looked like starved shadows had these words written all over them. Slaves forever to whisky. You ruined me, pointing a long bony finger into my eye. My gold was around my neck. I imagined I could see in my gold the faces of hundreds of my old neighbors' women and children. You ruined my husband, or father, and got his money. I thought I could argue or bribe my way into Heaven, on account of my religious baptism. I was the most responsible and respectable man in Hangtown. My name was good at the bank for any amount. So I knocked at the door. St. Peter opened it. Said he, 'What do you want? Who are you?'

" ' I am Brother Thomas who was converted and baptized twenty-four years ago on Spring River, Missouri.'

" Said he, ' Look at all that gold.' I did not want to do that, for I knew that I had not given value received for one cent of it. I had got it all for alcohol, and tobacco, strychnine, and other poisons called whisky. Said he, 'Look at it!' At this command I was obliged to do so, and there, in letters of fire, were the words, 'Robber, murderer, lying thief, whoremonger.' Said he, 'What is written of such?'

"'They shall be cast into outer darkness,'" said I. 'Out of thine own mouth will I judge thee.' Well, I believed, had faith, and was baptized.'

"'Believed,' said he, 'can a man have such a terrible array against him as that, and believe? What do the Scriptures say of him who says he believes, and does not obey?'

"'He is a liar, and the truth is not in him.'

"He slammed the door in my face and I fell back fainting. When I recovered consciousness, I was in somebody's arms. I thought I was in Abraham's bosom and lay there one moment deliciously happy. A voice said, 'Bring those red hot tongs and pull his toe nails off. That will bring him to.' I opened my eyes and found myself in the devil's arms.

"'Oh!' said he, 'my preacher tried to fool somebody! Did you try to fool St. Peter?'

"'You never fooled anybody but once, then you fooled old Brother Thomas. When you sold whisky, you said 'Well, if I don't do it somebody will; I might as well do it as anybody.' Every drink you sold made you a meaner man; made the distance between you and God and goodness greater and greater, until you finally got to be meaner than I, the prince of liars. You will keep on fooling yourself forever.'"

I had known Brother Thomas in youth, and was very sorry for him. He told me to tell his boys to stop their wicked ways and serve God. Here the beautiful woman came to me with a glass of clear, sparkling wine to drink. My old appetite was about to convince me that I could do so, and keep it concealed, when I said, "God have mercy and save me for Jesus' sake," and I awoke.

On awaking I commenced and immediately wrote my dream. I canvassed uninterruptedly two or three days for the *Prohibitionist*, returning to my room supperless. The question came up, What are you working for? Is it God's work you are in, or is it

3

of the devil, or is it a selfish aim? In answer, I say, I am one of a vast army of men, women, and children whose lives have been wrecked by whisky, and I want to see the time when it will be impossible for poor people to get it.

If we can get the United States constitutional prohibition and State constitutional prohibition, there will still be some whisky sold and drank. It cannot be thoroughly enforced any more than the law against stealing. There is a law everywhere against stealing; men break it everywhere and steal. Sometimes they are punished and sometimes they are not. The prohibition law can be enforced as well as that, and it will be as effectual as the law against stealing. Is it practicable? I believe it is. There are enough prohibitionists to-day to carry it, but they are not organized. The Republican and Democratic Party cry, we swallow up the whole people; there is no room for a third party.

I believe if we divide the Republican Party in the North and the Democratic Party in the South, the Prohibitionist is the party that will make a young giant who will fashion all things anew. So I decided. It is God's work. It is eminently practicable and an answer to the last question. It is as nearly unselfish in its purposes as any work in which men ever engage. If I keep in this work for God and prohibition, I am saved. If I engage in anything else, temptation to drink will sooner or later result in my downfall and ruin. With these reflections I fell asleep and again dreamed. At first strange faces and forms, penniless and weak, canvassing all day for my paper. Should I give it up and go to some better paying business? Old Abe and Singleton appeared alternately, first cheering words from old Abe, "Strike on, Massa William, right in the same place, the rock will break bye and bye clear through and through." Then Singleton would say, "You are a fool, there are a hundred agencies in San Francisco that would pay you better than this. Give it up. Make a little money to keep you from starving and then commence work on this. There are thousands of people here with great wealth, who do not think that the cold grave ever awaits them. Minister to their greed or selfish desires, or vanity; make yourself useful to their senses, like Bob Ingersoll. Flatter their vanity and they will bless you and pay you. You are engaged in a work of truth which makes them see themselves as they are. Now they will curse and rob you in return.

"One of their sons is at twenty-one years of age a splendid scholar, and with a large fortune started out in the world, without one single interest in common with the vast masses around him. Do you think that son has been favored by the seeming good fortune which has fallen to his lot? Is it possible, in the nature of things, for him to embrace the salvation of the meek and lowly Jesus? In his drives every day he sees thousands of struggling young and old men and women, terrible poverty making their lives an incessant battle to keep the wolf from the door. If he says anything it is, 'Am I my brother's keeper.' He takes a cold. The physicians can do him no good; brain fever hurries him to an early grave. Alone he crosses the dark river. He stands on the other shore; the shore of vast eternity. He has, strange to say, all his money; it is a witness against him. The thousand wants which he ought to have relieved are there. The truth, slighted and scoffed, as it fell on a thousand occasions, stands there. Neglected salvation through Jesus all there.

"'Lost, lost!' he cries as he views the terrible witnesses against him. He hurries to the presence of the devil. As he approaches, he sees his mother, the fine lady mentioned in the other dream. 'Oh mother! you never told me of Jesus and his wounds for our sake. You were in love with glitter and show and gold. Now in these scenes we are to live forever! Cruel, cruel fate!'"

Old Abe put in an appearance, and Singleton left. Said he, "You are writing down your dreams. Facts are stranger than fiction. The Scripture says the sins of the father shall be visited upon the children, even down to the fourth generation; on the other hand, the promise of God is to you and your children.

"A young man arrives in Hangtown in the fall of 1849, penniless. He has a blanket and a worn old Bible and song book. He passes his first night under a tree. By the light of his fire he reads an hour or two in his Bible before retiring. He then sings in loud, clear, ringing tones, a good old hymn; kneeling, he opens his heart to God in prayer and praise, and asks his blessing on his work in the new country. He rolls himself up in his blanket

and sleeps very sweetly. With early dawn he rises, builds a fire, reads a chapter and sings a hymn of praise, and again kneels and prays. When he arises he is confronted by another young man. 'Thomas Dunn is my name,' said the new comer. 'James Ross is mine,' shaking hands. Thomas said, 'I heard you singing that dear old hymn, my mother's, in Ohio, and I came to your camp to get acquainted.

"Said James, 'I am glad to know you but I have no grub to offer you a bite.'

"'Well,' said Thomas, 'come to my camp. I want a partner. I have a claim and mining outfit and will divide.'

"'Thank God,' said James.

"Their claim was a good one. They prayed, as they had been taught, and worked hard. Their habits were regular and God greatly blessed their labors. They were foremost in every work of charity, visiting and comforting the sick and afflicted. They rapidly acquired a very large fortune, notwithstanding their munificent charities. After relieving the wants of friends back East, at the end of two years they weighed their dust and found that each had $100,000 in gold. Their hearts went out in thanksgiving to God. For five generations their forefathers had been pious. They had often heard of the beautiful valleys around the bay. They gave up mining. Each had graduated as a law student before coming to California. When they arrived at the bay, in the fall of 1851, the whole talk was about jumping land. The valleys were covered with Spanish land grants. An old Mexican was in the city endeavoring to sell a grant of eleven leagues. He wildly cursed the Americans. He said he had a perfect title, having lived on the land forty years, and that the Americans had jumped every rod of it. He would sell the whole tract for $20,000. James Ross looked at the title, saw that it was perfect from the Mexican Government, found the records all right, and said, 'I will give it.' He notified the squatters of the transaction. They laughed at him, and threatened to lynch him. They all improved their farms the same as though there was no Spanish grant. In 1854 it was confirmed by the commissioners and by all the courts. The squatters were intelligent. A large town had sprung up in the center of the grant. The squatters were

prosperous. North, south, east, and west the courts were eject-
ing squatters. James Ross quietly watched events. He was
an exhorter, and held meetings in the school houses which had
been erected by the squatters. They well understood that he
could eject them by law. They also knew that a law firm in San
Francisco would have bought the grant from the old Mexican in
a day if Ross had not completed the trade, and that the law firm
would have ejected them by due process of law as soon as possible thereafter.

"In June, 1854, he summoned the squatters to meet him in
a certain town that had sprung up on the grant, in reference to
their homes. There were nearly a thousand persons present.
There were 400 homes on the grant. Ross read a letter from
Eugene Casserly, representing a law firm in the city, offering him
seven dollars an acre for the entire grant. They owned a grant
joining it, stocked with cattle, and needed more land. 'But,'
said he, 'I recognize one fact, and that is that every one of you
will be ejected from the land at once, and will have to leave your
improvements, which are considerable. I have to give an account
to God for everything I do. I own the land, bought it and paid
for it, and have a right to sell it legally, but I hold myself amena-
ble to a higher law. You are in the condition that God intended
all men to be, and that is the home condition. In the beginning
he made just so many facts or laws, and men are happy in pro-
portion to the number of facts discovered and practiced. In
thousands of countries and districts in the United States the land
has been divided up and the home condition established, result-
ing in the rapid development of the resources of the section so
settled. And, what was better, they always, without fail, built up
a superior manhood. I have studied this question in all its bear-
ings. If I sell this land to Casserly & Co., they will immediately
put 400 homes in mourning. You will all be involved in law.
Lawyers will fleece you. A miserable life for all of you will commence. When you are ejected, there will be no place for you to
go. You will scatter out into the different towns, which are already too full. Your manhood will be reduced to a lower level,
and your wives and children will at once feel the deterioration
A man with a home is the better the moment he comes in pos-

session of it. The nation is stronger the moment he comes in possession of it. The State, county, and district are all the better and stronger by the fact that he has it. On the other hand, the man and his family are infinitely lowered the moment he is, by any means, deprived of a home. If he sells it and gets the money, the effect of his losing his home is the same. The nation, State, county, and district are all injured. If it is so with one man, then how much will be the damage to the body politic in case of the dispossession of 400 families?' Said he, continuing, ' If you want your homes, appoint a committee of five to draw up the terms upon which you would like to buy?'

"The committee in due time reported that they were willing to pay $10.00 per acre for the land, payments to be made in one, two, three, and four years, with mortgages on the land duly executed and recorded as security. Interest at two per cent. per month until paid.

" 'Now,' said Ross, after all the papers were drawn up and signed, ' I want to make a speech. You are in the best climate in the world, a fine rich soil, and each one of you are at peace with all the world. You have beautiful homes. No man can estimate the value of these homes. They are yours. All modern progress rests upon the home power. That country without homes maintains law and order at a fearful cost. In fact, liberty lives nowhere without homes. One home is worth a hundred soldiers in the maintenance of law and order. God made the land for homes, and they are of vital importance to your happiness. Water is not more valuable to man's physical life than homes are to his moral life. All other countries on the earth but ours have standing armies, and when the time comes that the homes are all absorbed by the larger, which I very much fear is approaching, then we will have standing armies maintained at a fearful expense in money and morals. Your homes have a mortal enemy. Suppose an army with banners, guns, and ammunition were to at. tempt to quarter itself upon you, burn your fences, insult your wives, force contributions of provender, flour, hogs, poultry, butter, and eggs, you could organize, appoint your officers, procure war material, meet the enemy, and perchance drive him from your midst. If not, sacrifice your lives on the field of honor in the attempt. The enemy I speak of is worse than an army. That enemy's name is whisky. It is the enemy of homes everywhere. If you do not pay me for your lands it will be whisky. I will take your land back at cost for land and improvements at any time. I know you have a fine bargain.'

"The land rapidly increased in value. In 1855 the assessor valued wild lands at fifty cents an acre. An eleven-league grant joining the Ross tract, covered with wild cattle, only paid taxes on $50,000, everything counted. It was wild land. The Ross tract was valued by the same assessor, who had been elected in the interest of land monopoly, at $15.00 per acre.

The 50,000 acres, at $15.00 per acre	$750,000
Four hundred houses, barns, corrals, etc.	400,000
Every farmer had some fencing.	400,000
The wagons, teams, tools, etc.	500,000
	$2,050,000

Or about twenty times as much taxes paid by the Ross tract as that just like it but in the hands of one man. The man who owned the big ranch traveled in Europe, and of course spent his income there. The settlers on the Ross tract lined the roads with wagon loads of grain, hay, and poultry. They marketed immense quantities of beef, pork, mutton, and horses. They were buyers of newspapers, music, books, etc. Immense quantities of dry goods, groceries, teas, silks, shoes, and every merchantable article found cash buyers among the homes on the Ross tract.

"Is the city of San Francisco interested in the breaking up of land monopolies? Is there a tax-paying interest in the State but what is injured by it? Have not land monopolists from the earliest period of the State's history debauched the elective franchise in behalf of their own interest? I ask, are not the courts, the legislative and executive departments of the Government, all a living power arrayed in favor of land monopoly and against homes? From San Diego to Shasta there is one large tract after another. In all the valleys these tracts are large enough for 200 homes. An owner of a large tract employs say fifty men on an average. Are these men so employed the kind of citizens demanded by a great republic, or are they just such as can be used to destroy the nation's liberty by debauching the purity of the ballot-box?

There are no school houses on these large grants. There are saloons, which levy tribute upon the wages paid the employés.

"The devil accomplished the finest piece of strategy of his life when he argued the United States into annexing Texas. That was the cause of the war with Mexico. Through that war we acquired New Mexico, Arizona, and California. Not but what we added many millions to the circulating medium of the world by our gold fields in California. Not but what California is the best State in the Union naturally. The United States, up to the annexation of Texas, was engaged in building up manhood. Her home condition for 220 or 230 years was precisely that which God ordained from the beginning should never fail in building up manhood. If it had not been for that home condition we never could have had Washington and his armies, who fought seven years, and then, without pay, laid down their arms and resumed the various occupations of peace. The splendid pluck, grit, and endurance exhibited by the Northern and Southern armies were a result of the home power.

"Now a large portion of our country has culminated, and we are on the downward grade much faster than ever we went up. A standing army will be absolutely necessary to hold in check the wildly throbbing, beating heart of the vast mass of unnecessarily poor people who crowd the cities and towns of this State. If the lands of the State were divided up into homes, the cities and towns might be five times as populous, and not too large for the country. In fact, many others would spring up on every large grant, two or more towns in addition to what there are.

"James Ross, as he entered his buggy to drive to a farmer's where he intended to pass the night, was reaching for the lines when a drunken man fell heavily under the horse's feet. The horse sprang to one side, and, bounding forward, collided with a large wagon, capsizing the buggy and throwing James under the wheel of a moving freight wagon. It moved right on over his heart, instantly crushing the life out of him."

Abe continued: "Here was a man who had, in early boyhood, embraced Jesus. One who had never faltered in his allegiance. His head and heart and pocket-book were practically dedicated to God every moment. What was the result? God had made him wonderfully prosperous in this world's goods. Now, in the prime of manhood, he met with a violent death."

A halo of glory spread over Abe's face as he continued: " Without a moment's warning he was on the banks of the dark river. He knew that he was in the arms of the Almighty One. In a moment they were passing its dark and dangerous flood, and were safely landed on the other shore, where was gathered quite a multitude, and all shouted, 'Welcome, Brother Ross.' A voice more precious, and one that he well knew, said, 'Ye have been faithful over a few things; I will make you ruler over many.'

" I saw him," said Abe, " with the Saviour. The character formed on earth was to go on and grow under the immediate eye of Jesus through vast eternity.

" I must not omit to mention the best witness he had. Whenever he had been called upon for help in this world, if he did not know the merits of the case, he would say, ' In thy name, O Lord, this is casting bread upon the waters.' Now, here was the harvest, a multitude of the sweetest singing angels to sing heavenly songs as Jesus carried him to the mansion prepared for him."

THE OLD FORTY-NINER'S STORY.

The first I ever heard of California was in the year 1839. I was fifteen years old. We lived in the country. I went one night on a visit with a boy of my own age (fifteen years) who had a beautiful sister, with whom I was desperately in love. It is curious how hard a boy's first love goes with him; but the love of the girls has been a magnet shaping my whole life. I am sixty, and have ten living children. My wife, Mrs. H., and all the old women look like girls to me. Well, I went home with James Boring. That night when the old gentleman came in (he owned a plantation and a hundred negroes), he opened his mail and there found a letter from the Agricultural Department with a table-spoonful of wheat that had been raised in California. An old map musty with age was sought in order to find where the country was that produced such round plump wheat. The next I heard was after we moved to Missouri. Thomas H. Benton, the great Missouri senator, procured the passage of a bill to make an appropriation to pay John C. Fremont for organizing a company of a hundred men to cross the great American desert (there is no desert where that was marked) to California and Oregon as topographical engineer. His wife, Jessie, Mr. Benton's daughter, wrote a book which had a very large sale, composed from Fremont's diary.

It was thought to be the glory of any administration to acquire California. When Texas was annexed and war was threatened, the United States sent around the Horn, under Commodore Sloat, a naval squadron with secret instructions. James K. Polk, of Tennessee, was president. The councils of the nation were in the hands of the South. The South wanted California as a splendid area into which they could take their slavery. When Texas was admitted a condition was stipulated for a division of the State into four additional ones. The fiercest struggle was at that time going on to maintain in the Union a balance of power in the senate. The Northwest was rapidly improving and European immigration all went North. It feared competition with slave labor.

Sloat was secretly instructed to proceed to the Pacific Coast and the moment he heard of war between the United States and Mexico to open his instructions. England and France each, with the same thing in view, sent naval squadrons to the North Pacific with instructions, with or without a pretense, to get a protectorate over California. An agent of England had begged General Castro at Monterey to allow him to declare an English protectorate, but Castro declined, or hesitated a little too long.

All the aforesaid naval squadrons were in the harbor at Mazatlan watching each other. One bright morning about eight o'clock, without previous notice, the American Flag-ship with her two consorts were observed hoisting their anchors and getting ready to set sail. The French squadron commenced to get ready to follow the American and watch it; the English slowly following. The American knew exactly where it was going. The other two were determined to watch it. Fortunately, when outside, a storm separated the fleet. The American arrived in the bay of Monterey.

As soon as Commodore Sloat heard from U. S. Consul Larkin, of the effort of the English Consul to induce General Castro to ask an English protectorate, he at once went ashore and hoisted the American flag, issuing a proclamation in accordance with the secret instructions he had received. He said that the people would not be interfered with in any respect; that the same officers would enforce the laws they had always been used to; that property would be protected, and any one having the sales of title to land would be protected in it.

Commodore Sloat's proclamation had been written for him in Washington. That clause binding the Congress to protect those having a color of title to land was inserted in the interest of slavery. It was right, legally right, for the South to fight for slave territory. The death knell of slavery was to confine it. New cheap lands made a big demand for slave labor. It has always been the custom to denounce the laws of the generations preceding as barbarous. All nations have looked back to the barbarous laws and conditions of their ancestors to keep away investigation from themselves and their laws. If a man owned a hundred negroes, it was to his interest to see that they were clothed and fed, the Bible read to those negroes, and the doctrine of marriage, and the family, encouraged, for then fewer doctor's bills would be necessary for nameless diseases. They also in this condition raised more children. Then they were positively, by law and public opinion, protected from the whisky seller. It was a penitentiary offense to sell a negro whisky. True they had to work. The family by law could be broken up. The father sold one place, the mother another, and the children another.

One white man on a ranch in California to-day would do the work of three negroes in the South in ante-war days. The compromise of 1820 when Missouri was admitted into the Union gave all territory south of 36° 30', to slavery, but it did not settle up like the free territory North. Southern Statesmen determined to make slave States as fast as free, and California was needed and large land grants were to be established all over the State, so as to make it impossible for free labor to get a hold. No man who held slaves under the law was guilty of breaking any law, human or divine. The law was hateful and abominable. The law to

imprison a man for debt was just as bad.   The race made by the
naval squadrons from Mazatlan to Monterey was of the utmost
importance to the human family.   The authorities at Monterey
would have gladly welcomed the French or English in place of the
Americans.   Texas had just been annexed.   Fremont had de-
fiantly marched through the whole length of the State, and the
California authority would have gladly thrown itself into French
or English arms to obtain protection from the embrace of its
hated enemies, the Americans.   Thus you see it was obtained
first by conquest.   Then by the treaty of Guadalupe-Hidalgo,
by purchase.   Let us take two bird's eye views of California as it
it was thus obtained by America from Mexico.

A splendid eagle enters from the south representing slavery.
He says all these splendid valleys of rich new lands, already divided up into large tracts or grants by Mexico is the very thing we
need for our sons.   A splendid State after the order of the
patriarchs of old has been thrust upon us, almost without the
asking.   This is our natural heritage.   Another bird, the gentle
dove, enters from the north.   It says: "Homes, splendid heritage! Just as it comes from the hand of a most loving Father,
intersected by thousands of streams full of fish, its valleys,
plains, hills and mountains abounding in game.

This is the cradle of liberty.   Homes here will have an area
in which to build a manhood such as has never been witnessed.

Alas for human calculations.   The great plumed eagle knew
well that slavery owned American genius, all the offices of
Government, all the public press.   The pulpit of the entire
South, and nearly that of the entire North gladly prostrated itself
before the golden image of slavery.   Commodore Sloat's proclamation declaring that all in the possession of land, having a
color of title would be protected, forever binding on the Government just coming into possession.   Mexican script was only 25
cents on the dollar and with that 90 leagues could be bought for
$100; about 18½ cents an acre.

The three Hebrew children were again thrown into the fiery
furnace. If it had been thought that there was the remotest chance for
this Pacific State to be free soil anywhere in its future it would
not have been an American State to-day.

The naval squadron would not have been sent to the Pacific Coast to look after it. The dove was to be equally disappointed. It did not know that a new order of things worse than slavery ever was, could be devised and incorporated upon a new fair State which was so fair to look upon and which possessed a promise of a million homes and a superior manhood.

It was a virgin State. Thousands of herds of wild mustangs, with flowing manes and tails, roamed uninterruptedly where now grow unlimited fields of wheat and barley. Under the shade of the trees which grew on the banks of the rivers and creeks, bands of elk, deer and antelope lazily chewed the cud of contentment.

A death-like calm had not been disturbed for thousands of miles, north, south, east, and west. But hark ! what sound is that borne upon every breeze that seems to wake the nations? All mankind to earth's remotest bound rises with listing ear intent.

'Tis not pestilence, cholera, famine, nor war. These dread evils are always confined to a small area. Yellow fever may make New Orleans quake with fear, cholera might depopulate New York and London. Napoleon through war's terrible calamities make Europe put on sack-cloth and ashes and mourn fifty years, but all these are local. The world hardly knows anything about them when they are happening. Gold had been discovered at Sutter's Mill a hundred miles from the bay. For a thousand miles along the coast back of the bay of San Francisco, gold in large quantities is being dug. This discovery is more powerful than the tread of armies.

The noise of busy preparation to go to these new gold fields is more emphatic, and significant and wide-spread than any preparation for a campaign ever made by military chieftain. From every quarter of the civilized earth they come at terrible cost to life and purse. The rush was so wide-spread, frantic, senseless, and unprovided for, that millions fell by the way.

In the first four years from '49 to '52 inclusive, four million men started to these shores from every town, city and hamlet on the civilized earth. There were no means of travel and a million fell by the way. What can there be in gold to so move a whole world? Preachers from a hundred thousand pulpits eloquently described the ruin brought upon any people by an inordinate lust for money. They got down from the sacred desk and joined the rush. Doctors forsook a comfortable practice. Lawyers threw aside their briefs. Fathers tore themselves away from the care of little ones and the fond embrace of tender wives.

Thousands of love stories were acted out better than any romance ever pictured them on paper. College professors threw up their professorships. Education, improved mental attainments, makes nations, communities and individuals want money. Even religion, our holy religion, one of whose tenets is "money is the root of all evil," makes us want gold.

I would not give a cent for that man's religion which allows him to sit down and wait for God to feed him. Religion makes a man seek for gold to spread God's truth, to feed the hungry, to clothe the naked and relieve man's wants. Education makes a new want for gold, books, music, art, flowers, luxurious surroundings, makes a demand for gold such as the same man would never have if uneducated.

They crowded over every available route across the plains, wearily pulled themselves up the eastern declivities of the Sierra Nevada and dropped down the western slope into what?

The South sent up a herd of Mexicans, almost as many as the Americans. The world sent the largest fleet ever known on the high seas freighted with human produce. There were five hundred ships at one time in the bay of San Francisco without a sailor. This army by the sea met the other across the plains in the grand center of attraction, viz., the mines.

Here were a dozen civilizations, about three million of men without law or churches or women, with open, free gambling, whisky everywhere, no homes. Gold was in great abundance but nothing else. No gardens or farms to supply the miners with vegetables or fruits.

Race hatred and prejudice were often the foundation of severe conflicts. All the land divided up into large tracts which would soon involve the whole population which had come for homes, as many did, in law-suits had not all been settled yet in 1884.

The United States had been engaged in developing a peculiar manhood. For 250 years the matter-of-fact, utilitarian manhood of a class that looks first to self and self-interest, had been a peculiarity of the civilization. Homes, peaceful homes, about 160 acres in each, surrounded with other homes of the same size, hewn out of the forest. The jungle grubbed out, all seeking the protection of law without a constabulary and without a standing army to enforce order. The children of the United States had been accidentally, or led by the hand of God. Some believe the former. I had rather accept the latter. They were well fed on good meat and bread, vegetables and fruit, and not too much schooling, but sufficient for practical purposes. Here I must say that in this condition a nation, town, county or settlement is always blessed of God. They naturally have faith and feel and know collectively and individually that God's blessing is upon them. This is the seat of all benevolence. The people knowing well that God's blessing was only kept by loving one another, it was everywhere considered a solemn mockery for one man to advise another to reform or love God when he knew that man was in poverty and want. They first relieved a man's wants and then said God has given me his great love and pardon and I cannot keep that love and see his creatures in want. This made an inquirer. If a man gets a sack of meal because God loved the donor, he wants to know more about it. It is a new argument that has weight. The people of the United States were the most religious and benevolent that any civilization had ever developed. They were brave and liberal. It is selfishness refined to be brave and true and to give God all his due in praise and service. The greatest selfishness is to be perfectly unselfish. The greatest good a man or woman can do him or herself is to constantly lead a life of self-denial and cross bearing. The truth that tells most in one's own favor, is to be perfectly true to others. It is not only so once or twice, but for a whole life-time.

Now then, gentle reader, in 1849 there were 35,000,000 of improved developed manhood in the United States. From all that 35,000,000 manhood, was selected its very best material to pour down in the State three million. One million died from the many causes while on the way. Thousands of homes had been mortgaged to raise means to send the best qualified, morally and physically. Large numbers of loved ones were never heard from. When they landed at the mines, what was their surprise to find that all the civilized and semi-civilized nations of the whole world were heavily represented on the ground.

There was no stealing, there was very little crime. Every gulch was rich. Gold was more abundant than anything. One of the very strangest things was that where there was so much gold, there was so much real poverty. Vast numbers were sick with chronic diarrhea. There was no means of caring for such, and they died. Vast numbers did nothing but prospect. It was impossible for them to settle down to steady work. Everybody that traveled had their blankets. Tramp, tramp, everybody tramped. The ground under the trees was covered with vermin, so many people dropped down in the shade to rest, leaving, in the shape of a louse, a testimony that there they had rested.

What is the proof that the American emigration had a superior manhood? First, they were congregated in a thousand towns; half the population belonged to other and poorer civilizations. All were after gold, the most exciting and absorbing chase that ever engaged the attention in one place of so vast an assemblage. Of course interests clashed. All were armed, whisky was everywhere drunk. A vast majority gambled.

Judge Lynch established his court in a thousand towns, and no court from the foundation of the world ever made so few mistakes. He who committed crime well knew that in case of arrest and proof of guilt, punishment would be speedy and certain. In opposition to most of the foreign element, Judge Lynch ruled with a justice seldom praised enough.

General Riley, a military governor, without any authority of law, in 1849, issued a proclamation appointing a certain day for the people to assemble and elect delegates to a convention which was to form a State constitution. Where in history does any occasion arise for an exhibition of trained manhood such as this? In three weeks this disordered mass assembled and held an election, and quietly dispersed.

The delegates assembled and from copies of other State constitutions, copied one for California in three weeks. In this way a State was born as if by magic, with government for all classes, as perfect and complete as any old community in the world. This convention were all new-comers selected at random. Nothing in the whole history of man ever raised a manhood equal to such an emergency. Homes had been 200 years engaged in this task. A grand trial of the young giant's power was to be exhibited in the presence of the gods. His brilliant success commanded the profoundest admiration of a witnessing world. Here was a new State formed in six weeks from its inception.

An election was ordered to decide whether the new State with its new constitution should be accepted or not. At the same election the electors were to elect a legislature and governor according to the provisions of the new constitution. It was accepted. Thus before the people of the United States, or civilized world, knew anything about it a new State was born. The slave power which controlled the Government at that time resisted its admission, claiming that according to compromises made that all territory south of 36° 30' should be left to the people to say whether they would have slavery or not. The South was right. She had a right under existing compacts to demand a vote in the Territory.

It was a curious fact that the new State had been acquired by King Cotton for slavery, but it was more singular and took every one with the profoundest surprise that the child as soon as it was born became a man and refused to have slavery thrust upon it. The election for delegates, the assembling of the convention, the forming of a State constitution, the ratifying of the same by the people at the polls, forbiding slavery, took the whole matter out of the hands of those minds at Washington who had plotted other things for this splendid Territory. They, however, fought it in Washington. It was six long months before, under a compromise, California was admitted into the Union. Under the terms of that compromise, that one of 1820 was repealed. Judge Douglas contended that now with that old compromise repealed, the people of a Territory decided whether they would have slavery or not. The South, or slavery, got a decision called the Dred Scott decision, establishing slavery everywhere in the Territory. The South still hoped to get the southern half

4

of the State for slavery, the history of which will appear in
"Pioneer life in California." Reader take a bird's eye view of
that young State. Sacramento, Stockton, Marysville, and San
Francisco were new cities, houses of cloth, shakes and adobe.
The streets were full of goods, men and wagons and drays
through every avenue. The whole population was young men,
large, tall and strong. New, wide, well-beaten roads led in
every direction to the mines. Every mile or two a new hotel
sprang into existence, as if by magic. The whole of the United
States was terribly excited, hundreds of mortgages were recorded in every county in the United States, in order to raise
money to send the most trusted on to California. Very large
numbers in making their outfits had in view the business of
teaming on their arrival, so that horses, mules and cattle doubled
in value in consequence of the California demand. To have an
American horse or an American cow was quite an honor.

The mines were considered inexhaustible by everybody.
It was thought that the more they were worked for a hundred
years, the more gold would be taken out. In every gulch where
there was water there was a town; the improvements were often of
a permanent character. The old Mexican governors were still in
the country on their ranches.

In consequence of this vast rush to the mines, the bands of
cattle, sheep and horses, owned all along the coast, became im-
mensely valuable. Just think, a Mexican, Jose Maria Sanchez—
a hospital old fellow living on the Pajaro River, forty miles south of
San Jose, the owner, according to Commodore Sloat's proclamation, of three large grants—had for many years kept a hundred Indians at work, skinning cattle and laying out tallow. A
beef bringing $5.00 was a good animal, $3.00 being a
fair average. Now he owned, on the three ranches, more than
40,000 head. Before the mining discovery they were worth nothing until butchered. Now when driven to San Francisco or the
markets made by the rush, they were worth $50.00 each. A man
suddenly, as if by magic, changed from a pauper to a millionaire.
Whisky was everywhere; men suddenly grew rich everywhere.
The Legislature had legalized and licensed gambling. It was *the*
amusement, *the* grand occupation of many classes. It was the

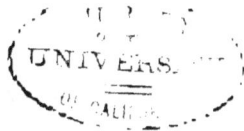

life and soul of the country. The bar-room of every hotel presented its tables to attract the eager, idle and covetous. Monte, faro, poker, every kind of game ran every day and night. Beautiful and well dressed women dealt the cards with exquisitely white and well-shaped hands. Lascivious pictures hung upon the walls. Lewd girls, freed from the necessity of all moral restraint, lounged voluptuously around bar-rooms. Such bar-rooms were vastly patronized. Music and blazing lamps gave great animation to the scene. No wonder the unwary visitor was tempted and fell before he had time to wake from the pleasing delusion.

To make a fortune by the turning of a card was delightful. The very men, glad hope and fear of eventual success was a charming excitement. For a moment men felt as great conquerors may be imagined to feel. They manœuvred on the green cloth—the field of their operations, thinking their own skill was playing the game when chance alone gave the result. At the end of a long evening's campaign of mingled victories and defeats, petty skirmishes, they would either draw off their forces to commence the game again the next day or hazard their all—thousands of dollars perhaps—on the issue of one great battle, and in a moment take leave of the table richer or poorer by a moderate fortune. Again and again were such campaigns fought and lost until the excitement and intense desire of play became chronic. When great sums could no longer be had, smaller ones answered the same purpose, and even in the end, lost like the others, gambling became a regular business and those who followed it professionally were really among the richest, most talented and influential citizens of the State. The sums staked were occasionally enormous. One evening $16,000 was called upon a faro table as a bet; the game lost. The money was counted out without a murmer. Twenty thousand dollars were often risked upon the turn of a card. The ordinary stakes were from fifty cents to five dollars, so that the ordinary day laborer could lay his moderate stake as stylish as a lord. The rich gamester became desperate. A half tipsy miner on his way East was the one who put the largest piles on the cloth. The bankers had no objections to these heavy stakes, they knew the game better than the players and were well aware of all the chances in their favor.

The extensive saloons, in each of which ten or a dozen tables run night and day, were continually crowded, and around the tables the players crowded three or four deep. The professional gamblers who paid great rents for the privilege of placing their tables in these saloons, made large fortunes by the business. Their tables were filled with heaps of gold and silver coin, with bags of gold-dust and lumps of the pure metal to tempt the gazer. The sight of such treasures, the occasional success of players, the music, the bustle, the heat, drink, greed and deviltry, all combined to encourage play to an extent limited only by the great wrath of the community. Judges and clergymen, physicians and advocates, merchants and clerks, contractors, shop keepers, tradesmen, mechanics and laborers, miners and farmers, were adventurers in their kind; every one elbowed his way to the gaming table and unblushingly threw down his golden or silver stake. While such scenes in hundreds of distinct places were night and day being enacted in public, the conspiracy in Washington to get California with the Mexican grants all in large tracts for slavery, was only too well plotted. The wild rush for the gold mines did defeat the hopes of the South for slavery, but it contributed largely to the help of the plotters to get the land. The plotters were to get control of public affairs in the politics, elect the courts and State officers. They were actually the State. The old Mexican governors and generals and keepers of archives were all in the State. They could make a land grant as well now as before the American acquisition. They covered every foot of the country, which was worth at that time anything, with large grants and made many float grants. Gwin was senator, elected to serve the Pacific Mail Steamship company. Fremont in the interest of land grabbers. He had a large grant covering the Mariposa.

Now, reader, to prove these facts, I will state that the country was in the hands of the Jesuits up to 1835. They owned from one mission to another, which were forty miles apart. A grant was never made till it was taken away from them. It took years to send to Mexico for a grant. The old soldiers of the mission were ignorant and composed the entire population. It was only eleven years between the time of the secularization of the country and the time when it was conquered. Of course any one can see there were but few genuine grants. They claimed to have 200. There were 800 presented to the land commission, appointed in 1852 by Pierce. It suited the purposes of the American plotters to at first fix these grants, good and bad, so that they would be universally confirmed. It then suited their purposes to have these grants all squatted on by the gold-seekers, so the politician proclaimed from every rostrum and stump. In consequence of this, men were elected, pledged to pass laws that would enable the squatter who entered upon land in good faith as a settler to recover on final confirmation to the grants for his improvements. The result was that all the land on the rivers and around the bay and on the coast was squatted on and recorded as pre-emption claims. Sometimes they bought land of a grant. There were often two or three titles to the same tract of land. The result was as had been intended. A perfect harvest of law-suits for lawyers and courts. Job said, "The earth is given into the hands of the wicked," which is no less true now than it was in his day. It is the standing complaint of the world. The moan of history is bad men in power. The land grant holders were necessarily compelled to hunt up witnesses to attend courts, to employ lawyers. The courts, lawyers, and attaches of courts were often the owners of games or put stock in the bank of games. The law suits were interminable. The consequence was as might have been expected, the Mexican grantees found themselves homeless by the time the battle was fought to obtain their homes. Now comes the battle against the squatters. They had only been led to go on to the land to annoy the old grantee. Suits are commenced for their ejectment. The squatters raise money to fight in courts which are too often parties in the suits. Judges are gamblers, lawyers are mental slight-of-hand performers. "Now you see it and now you don't." The American political system reached a greater depth of corruption in 1855 and '56 in California than it had anywhere else. The squatters' money was perhaps divided between the courts and attorneys. Decisions were made beforehand; they were ejected from homes which according to all principles of right belonged to them. The people were unacquainted with their leading men, and their officials were selected at random. The profits of mercantile transactions and mechanical labor far exceeded the salaries of most of the government officers which, beside as a class, were beyond the reach of men who would not bribe conventions and descend to low associations. The sudden and complete formation of the American government of California was not more wonderful than was the organization of the spoils system of party management under the lead of men who had received the highest education in political corruption before they left New York, which city furnished about one-sixth of the population of California, and a majority of those who controlled the dominant faction of the dominant party. All the arts founded or perfected by Tammany Hall or the Albany regency for defending the people out of a fair choice in the nomination of candidates. Party conventions were a farce. The vilest ruffians were employed by prominent politicians instructed to carry such and such wards. When election day approached, associations in the city were formed to sell their votes to the highest bidder. Gangs voted in every ward. The policemen were appointed to reward political service. They could be trusted for untiring labor in elections, but little could be expected from them in the matter of arresting criminals who had money or influence. The most dangerous criminals in California were themselves officials. Ten thousand homicides were committed between the years '49 and '59.

The crime upon the ballot box, the corruptions of the public service, the prominence of notorious criminals and ruffians and their patrons in city offices, the forgery of Meigs, the failure of the courts to administer criminal justice properly,—all these things had provoked the people who were engaged in money making to general desperation. It was impossible to reach and punish these crimes by law. What was the result? Before we discuss the result which was prompt and efficient for the time, go back with me to 1851. John Biglar as the Democratic nominee was elected governor. What did that election express? It clearly and forcibly expressed the dominant will of a vast majority of the people. That is that the land grants were nearly every one a fraud, and that laws should be passed protecting the squatters. The squatters were loudly promised protection by politicians who knew they had no power. The squatters were all powerful in politics. The land was all squatted on; it was worth nothing. Colonel Hollister bought the San Justo grant, near San Juan, for $20,000, containing 60,000 and 70,000 acres of land worth on an average to-day $50.00 per acre or $3,000,000. It was all covered with squatters.

The land commissioners were interested in the law's slow delay. In three or four years the courts and lawyers owned all the land. The processes were all arranged by which the squatters were to be ejected.

The squatters were the sufferers of the most trying and outrageous frauds ever perpetrated in the world's history. They were a class of men who made any sacrifices for law and order. A majority returned East, only to meet with disappointment. They never realized and the world does not to-day realize the fact that life in California in those days forever disqualified a man for a life in any other. Large numbers bought land only to get into lawsuits which have put many in their graves, many in insane asylums, driven many to murder. Large numbers were driven into the cities, towns and villages.

In 1856 the result arising from all the foregoing causes like a brilliant, unknown comet, sprang into existence. The Vigilance Committee, a body of citizens, took that law, which they themselves by their existence violated, pushed aside the officers who were themselves the criminals and executed, themselves, that law against all its violators but themselves. History does not repeat itself. This was a divergence from all precedent. The guilty were punished, the criminal element was overawed, the officials were forced to respect public opinion. They then turned that law back again to the officers of the law, gaining for themselves the plaudits of an astonished world. The land had all fallen into the hands of the few large holders. The people were driven into the cities, towns and villages. All had to engage in business of some kind. The vast majority were always poor in California. This is a strange anomaly. Whisky, gambling, lewd women did their work.

About this time a new discovery was made by the China companies. They imported large numbers of China women and, according to the laws of California, they were on every street, in every town, large and small, in the rooms most availably situated for their business. This lasted many years before it was repealed. California, is the youngest son sowing his wild oats, the prodigal who received his patrimony. The school fund was given to her by the United States. She contained 188,000 square miles. The sixteenth and thirty-sixth sections were all school lands. It was sold for $2.50 per acre. The proceeds were the school fund, they could not be diverted. The school system has been of a high grade from the first; the children have had superior school advantages.

No State in this Union, nor country in this civilization, has given any attention to physical manhood. Much has been expended by States and nations upon mental development. Vast sums have been spent to educate the mind, supposing the body to attend to its own development. A State never made a graver mistake. The first and highest duty the State owes itself and its citizens, is to prevent the monopoly of its homes, and by positive legislation bring about that state of affairs, or condition wherein all its citizens have enough land of their own from which a living can be made. Then they are in the condition or order in which God intended them to be from the foundation of the world. There are but few small sections of the State in the home condition. The climate, soil and mineral resources are unsurpassed. These are facts known perfectly everywhere in America.

A very large emigration has continued to pour into California every year from '49 to '84, a large number with means sufficient to return East in case of a failure to situate themselves pleasantly. A large number have come on account of health, arriving here almost penniless. The land, all in the hands of large holders, they have been driven into the cities, towns and villages, where their children have been educated. The children could not get work; Chinamen were imported to do the work; the parents of such children had moved into a circle of well-to-do, respectable people. The hardest task that ever fell to the lot of a poor, proud mother is to feel that she is, by her dress and that of her children, falling gradually below their condition. So a great effort is made to economize on every hand and keep abreast with the neighbors in appearance. The father may occasionally take a dram; every ten cents wasted is severely felt. The children when they come to the table find thereon just so much. The father divides it fairly and equally, the children go away half filled but satisfied. They have no cows to drive to the pasture, no pigs to feed or horse to water, but kill time by studying or reading till the school hour arrives for them to go to school. This is a description of one family. Day after day is repeated till a new generation is raised up. The children will be twenty-five or thirty pounds less in weight than the parents, and what astonishes the world is that they are not educated. Education like this does not educate only in one way, it makes a race of little, untrustworthy people. Now suppose the boys of such a family arrive at manhood at eighteen. The family has increased its natural wants. The father is getting old, increasing cares are laying a heavy hand upon his bending body. The loving mother says: "John," to her oldest son, the pride of the fond heart, "I am trying to work to help make a living, you are in need of clothing, don't you think you might earn something?" "Well, mother, I have been thinking I would like to try if I only knew how." The boy is very small, not well fed, in school all his life. There is positively nothing for him to do in or about his town; his best clothes are somewhat seedy. He starts out first in his own town. imported Chinamen are doing all the unskilled work, no one wants him. He often hears the words, "Don't want no d—n hoodlum in mine." He applies to every mechanic to get to learn a trade. "Don't want no boys in this county." Not a soul invites him to enter and tarry awhile and rest, no hospitable look or kindly word. At night he turns his weary way to find a tired father and mother and noisy brothers and sisters with not sufficient food for health and strength. At early morning, after discussing all the prospects through the night, he hopelessly tries it again. The hotel keeper says: "Johnny what are you doing?" "I am trying to get a job." "Well, you cannot do much, but come and work in the kitchen and I will pay you all you are worth." John is delighted. This hotel keeper's name is O'Brien. He has a son the same age of John, who has always attended the same school.

His bar-room is the center of attraction for the whole town; he has a small room attached to the bar-room, where there are two tables covered with a green cloth. Day and night men are gambling on one and often on both these tables. The bar-room has a peculiar language. All bar-rooms have. Nude pictures hang on the walls. Joseph, the oldest son, manifested a peculiar aptness in learning the language of the bar-room. Hideous monstrosities in the shape of men told yarns about the gentler sex that ought to have burnt out their tongues. Vulgar allusions, obscenities, is the language of the bar-room. The boy, as all boys will, greedily devoured these stories.

Well, Joseph had also graduated as an expert gambler, but secretly. It was not known generally in the town. The father whipped him nearly to death for drink, and he had not up to this time drank much. He and John slept together. John soon got to listening to the bar-room tales. It only took two weeks to make him listen with relish to vulgar anecdotes, and alas for poor human nature, in a month under the tutoring of Joseph he had graduated in a China house. Every night Joseph took John to a room where they played cards. He declared John was the best player he ever saw. John beat him every night. In about a month O'Brien said, "John I will pay you twenty dollars, you are a good boy, I will give you twenty-five dollars the next month." With what joy and gladness he took that money to his mother. Joseph stole a bottle of sweet wine and they occasionally sipped it. He was the stronger character of the two, besides he had always set down to a table well filled, and after he was done the table was still well filled. John soon learned to sip wine. Joseph was lavish with his money, always bragging about his winnings. He had let John win a dollar or so at every sitting during the following month. When he drew his pay for the second month, they went to their play before John could go to see his mother, and Joseph won all his wages in an hour. John was overwhelmed with grief; he went home in the deepest misery. The mother's ashy look of misery. She said "Your father will whip you terribly." John hid from his father. That night he went to Joseph and said, "Joseph lend me five dollars." "What for," with a look of surprise. "Well, I am going off, mother says father will whip me and I am going to run away." Joseph refused him—gamblers are the greediest, meanest men in the world. He had allowed John to win to bait him. John started off. We cannot follow him as he travels, turned from the door of cold, hard-hearted farmers, sleeping out in the chill night air. If hunger drove him to ask for something to eat, it was handed out like he was a dog. He at last got a job; he was called up at four o'clock in the morning, and with just time to eat his meals, he worked doing first one job and then another till eight P. M. He was too timid. He then crawled into the hay and shivered all night. Had this poor boy anything to do with the surroundings that made him a tramp?

The Sunday came. The family went to church and Sunday-school. He was manly and determined to stand it rather than tramp. The next Saturday the farmer paid him off at noon. "Well" said he, "let me stay until Monday, won't you?" "No; there's the hotel, half a mile off, go there, you have got plenty to pay your way." The poor boy went to the hotel, his board and lodging cost more than he had earned, what should he do? To remain was to be kicked out, there was no other resource but to tramp. He was well educated and good looking, but small; every one took him for a hoodlum; he arrived at the hotel. To his pleased surprise he was met by the landlord with great cordiality. At supper he declined to eat, just calling for a bed. He was pumped in regard to what he had been doing. They ascertained that he had worked two weeks for the rich farmer near by. They knew he had some money, so the landlord and his family treated him with very marked politeness. The next morning at breakfast he made the acquaintance of Frank Stevens, from Iowa. He said to John in a talk the boys had: "I am just out of school, I always had to work on my father's farm, doing chores evenings and mornings. I am strong, weigh 175 pounds and in good health, but would rather die than live in California three months longer as I have the last three months. I have not slept anywhere only in a hay stack and positively suffered more with cold than I thought it possible. I was a sober, Christian boy in Henry County, Ohio. It had for months been decided to send me to California as soon as I completed my

studies, so I came with just money enough to bring me here.
I landed in Sacramento the fifteenth day of October, 1883, with
one dollar.   I could not get work in the city; my one dollar was
soon gone; my trunk and clothing was pawned and soon gone.
Poor men told me of such dreadful suffering among farmers
that I feared to go to the country, but after two weeks I did, and
I have had barely enough work to keep soul and body together.
The farmers are brutal, worse than hogs.   If a laborer wanting
work asks for something to eat, they shove a crust of stale bread
and meat out of the door.   They are always pretending to be
afraid of tramps.   Never did people suffer like tramps, and never
was a class more maligned, and never on earth did any class of
men suffer so.   California makes men tramps.   The law threat-
ens to take them up for vagrancy, if they lay around the towns
doing nothing, and they have to tramp.   I have one dollar; I had
only one meal yesterday, and that is all I'll have to-day.   I
tramp, tramp, tramp, tramp, hunting work all over this State,
Sunday as it is, Christian as I am, I go to-day. "

John was crying.   Said he, " I have earned $15.00, don't go, I
will loan you a dollar to stay here to-day and go to church.   You
can pay me some day."   Frank gratefully accepted the loan as
his feet were very sore.   When he went to church he took a back
seat.   He wanted to pray and get near to God, but oh, the
leaden feeling at his heart.   It was too plainly perceptible that
that young fellow with his worn clothes was an intruder.   Not a
welcome hand from a single member of that congregation.

John would not go to church in his dirty old clothes.   The
landlord was very friendly, talking all the time.   His daughter
also paid him that attention and notice which a boy of eighteen
learns to prize.   John had been treated four or five times to
wine; it was very sweet.   Reader, that sweet wine is the most in-
toxicating drink a strong man can drink.   Drink of any kind
stimulates first the predominant animal passions and puts to sleep
the balancing moral organs.   With poor John the wine had stimulated his desire to get another place and make money, and had
put his caution to sleep.   The landlord's two pretty daughters
invited John to take a hand in a game of cards; he did so.   The
landlord said he would give the boy work at something, he

thought, the next morning.   Hope was thus inspired to help ruin the poor boy.   A small stake was proposed to make the game interesting.   After supper the game was renewed; John had been winner; they wanted their revenge; they all again sat down. John thought he had fallen into the hands of friends, he was very trustful and unsuspicious.   At ten o'clock when they began to get tired, by a few practiced tricks, they put up the cards, gave John big hands; the wine had destroyed his judgment and John was flat broke in half an hour.   The landlord counted the money, said he had won, and said, you want a bed.   "Yes, sir," said John, "but I have no money."   "Well, I give no credit, if you want a bed you must pay for it."   John said, "I have no money, you have got all I had in half an hour; you won't turn me out to freeze after winning my money?"   "The hell I won't.   Do ye's thinks I keeps beds for to give away to the loikes of ye's, either pay or go, I want to lock up."   The poor boy without a cent was turned upon the street, a cold January night, at ten o'clock. He now bitterly realized that the landlord was only carrying out with him a plan that had been successfully worked for years. This, dear reader, is just what California, the flower naturally of the Union, the garden spot of the world, has made herself—the manufacturer of tramps.

When Frank Stevens awoke he began to inquire for his kind young friend.   Frank Stevens was horrified when he awoke in the morning and found how they had robbed his young friend and turned him out in the cold.   He found his track and in a run he started after him.   About noon he overtook him; he was lying with his head on the root of a tree, asleep, his sweet face wet with tears.   Sobbing very hard, like a whipped boy, Frank knelt by his side and prayed for that poor, stricken boy as he had never prayed for himself.   He said, "O Father, he cannot work; no one will hire him, if he should get a job that taxes his poor frame to its utmost, some rascal of a whisky seller lays some plan to rob him.   His lot is a terrible one; have mercy; give the comfort of thy spirit."   As he prayed John opened his eyes. With difficulty he raised himself into a sitting posture.   Said he, "I was dreaming of my mother in the town of New York. She and my sisters were kneeling over me and praying for me.   I was sorry for my sins and wanted to be on the Lord's side, but oh, I could not. That old Irishman was so clever I did not think he would take all my money, even if he won it, and his girls with their sweet ways fascinated me and filled me with wine till my judgment was sound asleep. They filled me with wine till they were no longer amused; they then dextrously, as they had done a thousand times before, put up a few hands, giving me large hands so that I would bet. My mother and sisters were trying to pull me away all the time. I have acted over again in my dream what occurred yesterday and last night. " As he talked he slipped off a shoe, his foot was badly blistered. "O God, " says Frank, "what a country." A wagon was passing; Frank asked the driver to take John to the next town. He was a fine lordly farmer. A few years before, in 1849, himself had been a tramp, but now he turned up his nose, and said, " Do you think I keep a nice, fine wagon and team like this to haul tramps about in ? You must think I'm a d—n fool." Frank was large and strong. There was absolutely no work, he could not desert his friend, they were both very hungry. Frank took John on his back and packed him so as to get him on to the next house. He had the dollar loaned him and the half of his own which he had yesterday. It was a large grant, fifteen miles across it. John had traversed about half the distance in the desperate effort to keep from freezing the night before. To make the distance to the next ranch before night, desperate efforts were necessary. Despite their efforts night overtook them. Frank gathered a pile of wood, and by turning from side to side kept from freezing. John could hardly walk; they managed to get to the ranch the next morning. John bought some meat and bread at a fearfully high price, from an old woman who said the country was full of tramps, she had to feed them every hour in the day. John said, "I have not seen any coming down the river." "You haven't ?" They arrived in Sacramento that night and slept on the bare ground in the willows about the city. If they built a fire they would be seen and arrested. There is some religion and Christianity in the towns and cities, particularly among the American population, but the selfishness and inhumanity of the foreign element is horrible, particularly towards Americans. What has poor Americans done to incur such rancorous hatred of the Irish and Dutch? They are hypocrites and the well-to-do Americans never find out that such is the fact. They, in open defiance, ride over our American Sabbath and without hesitation would sell for five cents to a boy that which will wreck many lives. Many men who have ruined themselves and families trace their ruin back to five cents worth of beer bought of some Dutchman or Irishman. Their profession of religion and friendship and patriotism is a lie. The very same argument they use to present the immigration of Chinese we ought to use to place all foreigners on a level. Keep America for Americans. Let us build up on homes for all our people a splendid manhood. Tax lands held in larger quantities than a man can make productive. Let homes up to a certain value go untaxed.

www.ingramcontent.com/pod-product-compliance
Lightning Source LLC
Chambersburg PA
CBHW021527090426
42739CB00007B/817